Donna Nelson.

# THE POLLUTED POND: THE MYTH ABOUT AGING

by

Kata Lekich

A Hearthstone Book

Carlton Press, Inc.                    New York, N.Y.

I dedicate this book to my children: Andra, Cathy, Vinka and Mary. It's because of them that I've learned what I've learned between the ages of twenty-three and sixty, gotten the value from life that I have, and written this book.

A few years ago, when Cathy was twenty-seven, she asked me when it was that I first started noticing wrinkles on my face. I know she wanted me to say something like, "Well, I started noticing them at thirty and this is the magic thing I did about them so they wouldn't ever get any deeper..." I couldn't give her that answer, but she gave me the gift of knowing that even people who are thirty worry about aging. That was my inspiration to write this book.

I also dedicate this book to my wonderful and loyal clients, who through the years have given me the knowledge and experience to understanding myself and therefore others better, enabling me to enjoy and appreciate life much more.

# CONTENTS

# THE POLLUTED POND:
# THE MYTH ABOUT AGING

# 1.
# WHAT I'VE DISCOVERED

*Forty Years of People*

I've spent the past forty years working with people to enhance their appearance through hairstyles, makeup, color, design lines and general presentation. In those forty years, I've done a lot of listening.

I've discovered that there's one thing everyone fears, whether they are eight or eighty, and that is growing older. I've also discovered that there are specific reasons this fear exists, specific ways it gets started, and specific things you can do to avoid falling into the well of negative beliefs about aging.

This book is about making each day of your life more rich and exciting than the last, about the thrill of realizing all of your possibilities and potential, and about enjoying more life each year—no matter what your age.

Growing older is something we all do. We can't avoid it, but we can avoid some of the pitfalls—physical and psychological—that can make it a negative experience. We can, in fact, make it an extremely positive and joyful experience. We can let it be what it was meant to be: a time to enjoy the wisdom we've found, the love we've experienced, the excitement of creating each day anew, and the incredible richness of living.

I've always tried to provide an environment in which my clients could speak openly, honestly and freely about their thoughts and feelings. The 70,000 women, men and children with whom I've worked have taught me not only some of the pitfalls to watch for as we grow older, but some of the ways we can be more attractive than ever and enjoy life to the fullest every day of our lives.

*The One Great Fear*

Why do we have this pervasive fear of growing older? Some people suggest it's the fear of death, but I've found that very few people fear the actual experience of physical death. For the most part, they don't think about it. If they do fear death, it's usually because they're afraid they'll have missed some opportunities in life. "I should have stayed with my piano lessons and become a concert pianist." "I wish I'd been more loving with my husband, children, etc." "I always wanted to take a train ride across the country, and I never did." The regrets go on and on.

I believe the real source of fear about aging is something called the Polluted Pond. It's huge, pervasive, and so subtle we sometimes don't even know it's there. The Polluted Pond is the sum total of all the negative beliefs our society has about age and the aging process. It consists of unfounded beliefs like:

• Older people aren't as able, alert, attractive, useful, strong, competent as "the rest of us."

• Aging is debilitating, and older people can't take care of themselves.

• Older people are forgetful and frail. They can't be trusted, and they make us worry.

It's a long list, and we'll deal with it in more detail later. The problem is not just that this pool of negative (and often false) beliefs exists, but that it's swallowed whole and without question by people of all ages, so that it's constantly reinforced by children, peers, bosses, advertisers, and society as a whole.

The Polluted Pond affects nearly everyone, regardless of age, and sometimes the assumptions are so unconscious that we don't even know we're making them.

I've watched people see one wrinkle, or two extra pounds, and jump right into the Polluted Pond. They buy into everything there, accept all the negative assumptions and beliefs about people who are "older," without even stopping to examine whether any or all of it is true for them. All of a sudden, they think they're "old"—and you know what *that* means!

If they have a few grey hairs, they assume racketball is "not for them" just because it looks vigorous. After all, grey is "old," and "old" people don't do vigorous things. Their children are frightened for them if they live alone, and start treating them like semi-invalids, even if these people are in great health—and some of them are in better health than their children!

I'm not saying we don't need to be sensible and prudent, but I am suggesting that we don't have to think of ourselves as "old" and buy the whole Polluted Pond just because we're no longer sixty...or forty...or twenty. We need to examine our own situation and tell the truth about it, but we don't have to buy a whole bill of goods and limit our possibilities in life just because we have a certain physical characteristic or a certain number of years after our names.

Most of the assumptions in the Polluted Pond are about "old people," but we can start feeling old at any age. I've known twenty-five year-olds who thought their lives were over. "The problem of growing older" can be as difficult for people in their thirties or forties as it is for people in their fifties, sixties or seventies. It's all in the point of view.

In the course of the book, we'll examine how the Polluted Pond works, where it comes from, how it grows, why we can fall in at any age, and exactly what we can do about it.

### Where We Are Going

Our conversation will be about the various ways we can react to the Polluted Pond. We can fall in without putting up much of a fight, or we can take charge of our attitudes toward it and our responses to growing older. If we take charge of our lives, there's no way we can fall in. Personally, I'd like to see so many people taking charge that the pond is annihilated by the year 2000.

We are not talking about necessarily looking younger, though that may be one of the results. You don't *have* to look younger if you're not wallowing around in the Polluted Pond. You can enjoy the way you look now, enhancing what you choose to enhance, and let your own natural beauty shine through.

In the course of our conversation, I'll share with you the tools I've learned for living a fully, exciting, vibrant life at any age, and having more fun with each year that passes. We'll talk about:

• How attitudes can, quite literally, create your reality.

• Specific steps you can take to counteract the Polluted Pond.

• How people get tricked into thinking they're "older," or less than they really are, and what you can do to avoid this.

• Why the fear of aging can be just as debilitating for people in their twenties as it is for people in their eighties.

• Action steps—specific things you can do to look and feel your best at any age.

• How to look younger and more beautiful by letting your hair get grey, rather than struggling with the expense and aggravation of tinting, when tinting is no longer appropriate.

9

• Ways to appreciate and enhance your own natural beauty, rather than trying to hide "imperfections;" to let go of diminishing beliefs about yourself and remember that you're in charge; to take a stand for yourself and create, rather than limit, your possibilities.

• Trusting your own instincts and creating a personal style that's unique to you.

Lastly, you'll learn the SEVEN SECRETS I've discovered for living joyfully and creatively, free from the fear of aging. These seven secrets have completely altered and enriched the way I live and the way I grow older. They are precious to me, and I hope they will be useful to you.

We'll talk about a way of relating to yourself and the world based not on fear, avoidance or resignation...but on joy, love, appreciation and creativity. If you can do that, the Polluted Pond can't touch you. You can look forward to each new day as a chance to be and express more of yourself, a chance to revel in the wonderful gift of life.

I think life is too short not to be appreciated fully; too short to waste time on negativity, anxieties and fears; too short to stay stuck in old patterns or to buy into things that aren't true for us.

*Living Fully*

I don't believe that life is about diminishing ourselves and "winding down." I believe it's about being and appreciating all of who we are, getting wiser, and living more fully. To me, living fully means exploring and realizing as much of our potential as we can.

My ideal world is one in which all of us realize our own beauty and power, in which we all become the best that we can be and live up to our greatest potential.

That's what I've always wanted for my clients, and it's what I want for you. With my clients, it's been a gradual process of chipping away at pieces of negativity about themselves that they've picked up over the years. Sometimes they do this in a moment, just like that, but more often they take one step at a time, peeling off one layer after another until they realize that the most beautiful, wonderful person they could imagine—the ideal they've always wanted to be—has been there all along. It was just crusted over with a sense that somehow they weren't all right the way they were—and some splashes from the Polluted

Pond.

They discover that having thin hair or a nose that's "too big" doesn't have to stop them from being beautiful, vibrant, valuable people, and loving every minute of their lives.

This book is about getting a sense of your own natural beauty and your own power. Everything in nature has its own harmony and resonance, and strives to live out its full potential. Look at the sky, the sunset and sunrise, mountains, rivers, oceans, animals, flowers. We are a part of nature, too. Why should we be less beautiful and perfect? We are just as naturally beautiful and powerful as anything else in nature. We just need to realize it.

We do have one thing that some other things in nature don't have—a rational mind. That mind is a wonderful thing, but it can also be our undoing if we use it only to judge and criticize ourselves. This is not the use for which it was intended. Our minds are supposed to serve us, not to diminish us. Sometimes, though, they get a little out of control. They race around judging and criticizing until they've created something like the Polluted Pond. Fortunately, we can use those very same minds to undo the damage and set up a situation that lets us live in joy and freedom.

*My Own Experience of Aging*

For a good part of my life, I felt insecure about not having a college degree. I felt I didn't have much to say, and that what I did say was awkward and boring. I didn't trust that what I knew was worth anything, and didn't value my own opinions.

In my work, I was constantly coming in contact with people who were prominent in some way—very rich, very social, very intellectual, or very "something" that I was not. When a woman who was a lawyer sat down in my chair, I'd freeze—or I'd try very hard to cover up my insecurities and prove I knew something worth knowing.

Then I realized something. This lawyer didn't know anything about the things *I* knew about. She felt as helpless and uninformed about my industry as I would have felt in a courtroom. I knew a *lot* about my business, and was always learning more. The more confident I felt about what I did, the more I was willing to venture out slowly and into other fields, to try out my opinions about other things on people I considered to be much more educated than I was.

The more I trusted my own opinions, the more I found out

that they were valid, and that people were interested in them. They weren't always *right*, but I had a right to them just as everyone else had a right to theirs. The more I trusted myself, the less it mattered what other people thought. I'd freed myself from other people's opinions, and *that's how I found out the secrets of aging beautifully and enjoying more life each year.*

Starting to crack those thoughts gave me the key. It didn't matter what my insecurities were about. They could have been about my looks, my I.Q., things I'd done or hadn't done—anything. The point was, I started realizing that they weren't the truth. They were just my fears. I didn't have to live my life around them. They didn't have to limit me.

I was the one who'd set them up, so I was the only one who could do anything about them. I could either give them power—or not. When I chose not to let them run me, I won my freedom. It didn't matter whether I was dealing with the lawyer in my chair, or with the whole Polluted Pond—I didn't have to be at the mercy of my own insecurities.

Our insecurities are the foundation for the Polluted Pond. If we're stuck in our fear and uncertainties, we'll fall in every time. If we're in the habit of thinking negative thoughts about ourselves, and then we come upon the pond, it'll be the most natural thing in the world to fall in.

Fortunately, there's a way to reverse this process. Just as we build the foundation for the pond with our negative beliefs, we can tear down that foundation by identifying and reversing those same beliefs.

When we look carefully at how we built that foundation, at all the little pieces of steel and concrete that went into it, we understand that we're the ones who put it there. That means we're in a position to take it down. It's not just something that's "there" and we can't do anything about it. We chose it; we can unchoose it. That's what this book is about.

*No Ostriches*

Some people tend to adopt an "ostrich response" to aging. They don't want to think or talk about it, but somewhere in the back of their minds they're always worried about it. They've thought about doing something, but felt embarrassed or uncertain about what to do.

12

They don't feel important or deserving enough to take positive steps to improve the quality of their lives, or to enhance the way they look. They think that's for people who are richer, or know more about fashion, or more prominent, or who have more status, or who are good or wise enough to do the right thing. None of this is true.

Each one of us has a right to be all that we can be, and to enjoy life to the fullest. We just need to pick up the reins. More life each year is our birthright. All we have to do is claim it.

## 2.
## ATTITUDES AND APPEARANCE

*The Grass Is Always Greener*

Before we talk specifically about attitudes and aging, it's important to understand that our attitudes *always* have a tremendous effect on how we look—no matter where we are, what we're doing, or what our age.

I'm always amazed how few people are really happy with the way they look. At least, very few of them will *admit* that they are happy. No matter what we look like, or how old we are, it seems that most of us want to look different from the way we look. We think we'd be more attractive to friends, to children, to members of the opposite sex, and to society in general if we looked some other way—if we had a smaller nose, if our eyes weren't so close together, if we were taller or shorter, plumper or thinner.

This dissatisfaction can range from mild disappointment with the length of our eyelashes to a deep, oppressive hatred of something about our face or body. All these little dissatisfactions grow into a constant state of frustration and discontentedness about the way we look, and eventually become so much a part of us that we don't even recognize them.

The irony is that this constant frustration and discontent actually *can* make us less attractive. Ask yourself which person you would rather spend time with—someone who was generally content with themselves and how they looked, or someone who always seemed worried and unhappy about themselves or their appearance.

When we concentrate continually on what's wrong with us,

on the hair that should be thicker, the lips that should be fuller, the body that should be thinner it's practically impossible to be certain, confident, satisfied and joyful—and these are the things that really do make us attractive to others.

## Competing with Perfection

Until recently, we were rarely allowed to see anyone on TV, movies, magazines or ads who was less than perfect. Even the frazzled housewife undone by an inferior floor-scrubbing solution had a perfect oval face, flawless makeup, hair that had just received four hours of undivided attention, and the body of a 16-year-old athlete. Those of us who weren't born perfect, or had less than two months to prepare for a 30 second performance, might as well cross ourselves off the list of people who had right to exist on the planet.

Ideas of what "perfection" is have shifted from Lana Turner to Marilyn Monroe to Twiggy to Brooke Shields to whomever, but there has always been some ideal—and precious few of us have lived up to it.

In the past ten or fifteen years, we've begun to see some "real," imperfect, down-home people in the media. This is great for people who are ten or fifteen years old, and who've grown up seeing less than perfection on the screen and in the ads, but what about the rest of us who were trained and conditioned for the first twenty, thirty or forty years of our lives to believe that there was a perfect person out there, an ideal that was "beautiful" and "right"—and that we weren't it?

Do we have a right to life and happiness even if our face is "too long?" And what is "too long?" How long is a piece of string? Whose standards are we following here? It can get very confusing. Even if we completely rejected the way we were and aspired to the ideal, which ideal would that be? Lana Turner or Twiggy? Grace Slick or Linda Evans? Should we gain ten pounds, or lose ten pounds? Should we wear more makeup, or less? Go for a romantic look, or get a pink-and-orange mohawk haircut?

It's a game that can't be won. No matter what you do, there are perfectly valid arguments for doing just the opposite...if you're buying into the idea that there is some perfect way to be and are trying to fit yourself into that mold. You can't please all the people all the time.

*I'll Be Okay When...Or If...*

Each of us knows the feeling of thinking things will be fine *"when..."* or *"if..."*

When I get the new car...

When I get the right mate...

When I lose ten pounds...

When my hair grows out...

If I were younger...

If I were richer...

If I live in the right place...

It all boils down to: "I'm not all right the way I am."

Somehow, it's never okay to be just exactly where we are *right now*. Happiness, fulfillment, okayness are always somewhere "over there," just out of reach.

Aside from keeping us in a perpetual state of not being okay, this attitude actually keeps us *stuck* where we are. The more we resist whatever seems to be wrong, whether it's the way we look or the way we are, the more attention we give it, then the more it grows. By resisting it, we actually make it persist...and even grow bigger.

Ask anyone who has had a weight problem and tried to diet. The more they worried about their weight, the more attention they gave it, the more it seemed to stick. They were always thinking about what they were going to eat, what they weren't going to eat, whether they'd gained or lost a pound. They dieted, and then they binged. The more they worried about their weight problem, the more it seemed to persist.

The key is to give yourself permission to be exactly where you are, and who you are, *right now*.

*Living in the Here and Now*

What happens when you imagine giving yourself permission to accept yourself completely, right now, just the way you are?

Some people get frightened, because they think they'll stop growing and improving. They think they'll get complacent and turn into slugs or marshmallows. Not true. In fact, giving yourself that kind of permission may be the only way to move and grow. When you stop resisting something, you open up an opportunity to move on.

Not only that, but living in the here and now, rather than

believing that life will be better "if..." or "when..." is a lot more fun and relaxing than living with the burden of having to be or do something other than what you're being or doing.

The other flaw in the "over there" syndrome is that you can never win if you play this game where age is concerned. You can only be the age you are right now. If you're forty, and want to be twenty or sixty, good luck. You'll eventually get to sixty, but do you really want to spend the next twenty years waiting? And you will never, ever be twenty again...at least in this life.

When I was forty, I used to think, "Oh, if only I were twenty again!" Well now I'm sixty, and forty looks pretty good to me. I wish I'd appreciated it more when I was there, rather than worrying about not being twenty—especially since there was no way it was ever going to happen. All that worrying was just wasted time and energy.

I'm sure not going to wait until I'm eighty to appreciate being sixty! I'm going to relax and enjoy it. I'm going to appreciate it *now*.

### Attitudes Affect How We Look

Have you ever noticed that when someone thinks they have a large nose, that nose *actually seems to grow larger?*

Maybe it's because they're always talking about it. Maybe it's because they're silently self-conscious about it. Or maybe it's just some kind of undiscovered law of physics, that makes things seem to be more of whatever you think they are. In any case, we always seem to pick it up. I've seen it happen over and over with my clients, my friends, and myself.

I've had people come in and talk about nothing except how their hair had to be cut to hide this terrible nose or his double chin. When I looked at them, their nose or chin didn't seem strange at all, certainly not as strange as some other things. They were so convinced, however, and kept all those negative beliefs so firmly in place by repeating them over and over to me, that by the time we'd finished, I believed all those horrible things about their nose or double chin, too. It had become a self-fulfilling prophesy.

Obviously, it doesn't have to be a nose or a double chin. It can be anything about yourself or your appearance that isn't all right with you. If you carry those beliefs around with you all the time, building your own and other people's expectations around them, then you perpetuate precisely the things you'd like to hide.

I could have let thin hair run my life. Sometimes I still look at myself after washing my hair, and it looks like I have three hairs on my head. I don't, however, crawl into beauty salons like my friend Carol used to, apologizing before the stylist even had a chance to look at her, "Oh, I'm so sorry. I know I have the worst hair in the world. Everyone tells me so. I know it's the worst hair you've ever worked on. I'll leave quickly, quietly, right now if you want..."

All that did was make her feel even worse about her hair and set up a situation in which the stylist could do *anything* and it wouldn't be his fault. No wonder she never got good cuts.

Once Carol stopped clinging to the idea that she had "bad hair" and making sure everybody knew it, there was nothing to stop her from being a vibrant, alive, beautiful woman—even though she had thin hair.

### The Secret of Being Beautiful

By the same token, I know people who have far from perfect features, but are somehow beautiful! If you saw a still photo of them, you might not even notice them. When you see them in person, however, all those little "imperfections" fall away and everybody thinks, "Boy, is he or she attractive!"

It may have nothing at all to do with the way they look. It may be all in their attitude. Maybe they *feel* beautiful, or maybe their energy is so enthusiastic, warm, and open that their face and body actually appear more beautiful.

They are attractive because, for whatever reasons, they "attract·"

It's almost impossible to underestimate the importance of attitude. Our beliefs—about ourselves, others, and the world around us—are actually visible in our faces and bodies. They tell everyone exactly how we think and feel. We may be able to cover it up in odd moments, when we're really trying, but it doesn't work for long. People may not even know exactly what it is that makes them feel so good, or bad, around us—but they know how they feel.

What people see is partly physical, and partly the energy around us. We all project different levels of self-acceptance and aliveness. If we feel fantastic and gorgeous, people know it. If we feel too fat or too thin, our hair won't seem the right color or the proper cut. We protect the feeling that we really don't deserve to have a place in the world, and people latch on to this feeling quickly.

They may not be able to put it into words, but they'll sense the feeling—and that will be their most lasting impression of us.

That's why all the makeup, hair coloring and styling, and plastic surgery in the world won't help unless we begin from the inside out. That's the most effective and least expensive way in the world to be beautiful. We've all seen women who were impeccably groomed and had obviously spent a lot of time and money getting themselves together, but their faces were masks of pain.

One of the most beautiful women I know is seventy-two. She has wrinkles, and she looks seventy-two, but she has a twinkle in her eye and is one of the most alive people I've ever met. She's sure of herself, does as she pleases, is delighted to be alive, claims her place on this planet, and leaves in a month on a trip around the world that includes a stop in Russia. I hope to be that full of life when I'm seventy-two. She doesn't worry about whether or not she's okay; she just assumes she is and goes about her business, bringing joy to herself and everyone she touches.

The key, of course, is to accept and support yourself exactly as you look, and exactly as you are *now*, in the present moment. So you have thin hair, or wrinkles, or ears you think are too large or too small? Who cares? That's not who you are. Are you going to let that rob you of being a wonderful, alive person and enjoying life to the fullest? Do you want your life to be about hair and wrinkles and ears?

This doesn't mean you can't wear makeup, or have your hair done, or enhance your own special beauty in any number of ways. It's just that the more you appreciate yourself and your own uniqueness, both internally and externally, the more other people will appreciate you.

*SECRET #1:* ACCEPT AND LOVE YOURSELF.

Let go of diminishing thoughts and opinions about yourself, self-criticism and feelings that you aren't all right just the way you are.

Life is not about diminishing ourselves. We are meant to know, accept and love ourselves—physically, emotionally, intellectually, spiritually, and in every way. This doesn't mean we can't always enhance what we have, or present more of who we are. It just means we can take ourselves off trial, give ourselves a break, take a chance on ourselves without any strings attached.

## 3.
## ATTITUDES ABOUT AGING

*The Day They Tried to Make Me "Old"*
The first time I became consciously, dramatically aware that people consiered me "old," was at a big event produced at a local college by a group with whom I was involved. We were all outside setting up bleachers, tables and booths for about a thousand people in this huge park the size of a football field.

We spent the morning moving around enormous tables and pieces of lumber, and I'd been doing at least my share. We were always switching partners and working with different people, but I noticed that the same thing kept happening no matter who was carrying the other end of the table.

I'd pick up my end and we'd start moving across the field. After about four yards, the other person would turn around looking very worried and ask, "Do you want to rest?"

I was absolutely dumbfounded. I felt great. I wasn't even tired, so I couldn't imagine why people kept asking me if I wanted to rest. Then I realized that most of the people there were much younger than I was. As soon as they saw my grey hair and a few lines on my face, they made all sorts of assumptions about my energy level, my strength and my stamina.

They assumed I didn't have the stamina that they did, that I wasn't as strong as they were, that I shouldn't be expected to do the same things, and that I was in that way inferior. They meant only kindness and respect, and probably weren't even aware of what they were thinking, but it made me realize that no matter how generous or wise we are, we all have a certain set of beliefs about what happens to people when they get older. These young people bought into the Polluted Pond.

That experience hit me hard because I realized that even these nice, open, loving people saw me a different from themselves, and that they were making a lot of assumptions about me on the basis of grey hair and a few lines. It shocked me, but it brought the whole idea of the Polluted Pond to the surface.

## What People Believe

Here's a list of commonly held, and sometimes unconscious, assumptions people make about aging. I'm sure you can make your own additions to it. Without even realizing that they are doing it a large portion of our society believes that older people are:

• Less alert, energetic and competent, and therefore less trustworthy.

• Frail, debilitated and physically helpless, so they have to be "looked after."

• Forgetful, and therefore dangerous to themselves.

• On their way out and running out of time, so why bother with them?

• Unattractive and depressing.

• Not able to contribute much, personally or professionally.

• Either deaf or blind, or *going* deaf or blind.

• Sad and resigned...or at least they *should* be.

There's an underlying notion that older people have run out of steam, run out of time, and run out of opportunities, that they're just marking time until it's over, and often are burdens to their families and to society as a whole.

I'm not saying we can't accept help and kindness from others, or be gracious when someone offers us a seat on the bus, but I'd like to think people were doing these things strictly out of kindness and respect, and not because they thought we needed them or couldn't get along without them.

Sometimes we ourselves are the worst offenders. In the face of these nearly overwhelming beliefs, it's easy to get embarrassed and resentful. We pretend that none of it is true about us, rather than examining carefully what may be true and what definitely is *not* true. We fall right into the pond and invite others to treat us as helpless and inferior. It's one thing for others to categorize us; the real trouble starts when we start categorizing ourselves.

I refused for years to wear my glasses, for instance, because I was afraid people would see me as old and assume that, because I was wearing glasses and was therefore old, then all the other things on the list were true about me as well. It's not likely that anyone really would have thought that. I see kids running around in their glasses all the time. It was just that *I* had the notion, less than perfect eyesight made me "old," and that's ridiculous! I bought in completely, and got caught in the trap.

## The Polluted Pond

The Polluted Pond is that vast reservoir of beliefs about being older that includes everything on the above list and more. It includes any belief, assumption, opinion or point of view that points to growing older as a negative experience. It's deep, unconscious, subtle, and very tricky.

It won't do any good to march and picket against the Polluted Pond. Resisting it only makes it stronger. In the greater scheme of things, the Polluted Pond is probably neither bad or good. It's simply *there*, like the air, but that doesn't mean we have to fall into it. We don't have to let it run our lives, and no one can push us in unless we let them. In fact, just knowing the pond is there helps keep us from falling in.

When you're dealing with the Polluted Pond, it's hard to separate one belief from the other. Everything in the pond sticks together, and the waters can get pretty murky. It's easy to get confused. We look into the mirror and see one wrinkle, one sag, one grey hair, and before we know it, we've fallen into the pond.

When that happens, we not only have that one wrinkle, that one sag or grey hair, but we've gotten tricked into believing that it make us *old*. If we're *old*, then everything in the whole pond must be true about us. And every belief in the pond says we're less than we were, and should start thinking about throwing in the towel.

If you get a little arthritis, for example, does that mean you can't hear anymore? Of course not...unless you start believing that you're old and that old people can't hear. Does it mean you can't cross the street by yourself? Probably not. You may want to see a doctor and get whatever relief you can for the arthritis, but it doesn't mean your life is over.

If you have grey hair, does that mean you can't live alone? Maybe yes, maybe no. Only you can tell, but you probably shouldn't make that decision on the basis of your hair color.

One reason it's so easy to fall into the pond is that we're afraid all those other things *are* true about us. The minute I catch myself

21

turning my head to one side in conversation, for instance, I'm afraid I'm getting hard of hearing. There's absolutely no evidence that I am, but that just happens to be one of my fears. What I need to do, if I'm really worried, is go have my hearing tested, rather than just assuming I'm losing it because I'm getting older. The Polluted Pond can be like dominoes falling...one pushing the other, pushing the other, pushing the other.

I'm not saying that if you're ninety-eight years old, you ought to live alone in a tent, shoot your own game, run twelve miles a day, and to hell with anyone who tries to help you across the street. Of course we want to be prudent, and assess carefully where we need and want help. I'm just warning against buying the whole package just because you need bifocals, or because you don't feel as strong as you once did.

And I'm not just talking about people who are over fifty. These same things go on with people who are twenty, thirty and forty. The sets of beliefs may be a little different, but younger people are not immuned. People can start believing all the "old" things about themselves if they're twenty and five pounds over-weight, if they're thirty and not married, if they're forty and have no children, if they were passed up for a promotion, if their niece started college. It can be *anything*—as long as they think it makes them feel old.

The key is to *examine each item in the pond for yourself*, and don't take on anything that doesn't fit you. Remember, they're all just beliefs. None of them is necessarily true.

*Why The Polluted Pond Is Tricky*
The pond is tricky for three reasons:
1. You can get ninety-eight beliefs for the price of one.
2. These beliefs can be very subtle, almost hidden. People sometimes don't even realize they've fallen in until their heads are about to go under.

My friend Linda was one of these people. Linda is a wonderful, active person, a role model for all of her eight children. None of them thinks of her as old. The trouble is, she's starting to think of *herself* as old, and so anything they say, she interprets as a statement that she's not what she used to be.

Her daughter took her shopping recently and, as they were getting back into the car after a great afternoon, her daughter said, "Gee, Mom, I didn't realize you still liked to shop!" Linda replied, "Well I'm still capable, you know!" The daughter hadn't meant to suggest that she wasn't, but Linda's foot had slipped into the pond without her realizing it.

3.     The pond sets up a framework of *Limited Possibilities* and *Missed Opportunities*.

Any belief that diminishes us limits our possibilities and our options in life. Diminishing beliefs make us feel that we're less than what we were, instead of letting us enjoy being more than what we were. They also set up a climate of fear, fear that we've lost opportunities to do things and that those opportunities will never come again.

I used to assume that people were afraid of missing careers, relationships, children, trips, leisure time, etc. That's not usually the big one, though. The main thing people tell me they're afraid of is that *no one will ever really understand who they were*, deep down. Sometimes women tell me they've lived with a man for forty years and raised five children, and they don't think any of those people really know them. They know the "mom" or the "wife," but they don't know the person. If I had to pick the one deepest fear that people associate with aging, it would be that.

*What You Can Do About It*

I know a woman who is wonderful at weeding out negative beliefs. It's almost a hobby with her. She thinks of herself as a garden, and of negative beliefs as little weeds she needs to keep plucking out so that the flowers can grow big and beautiful. She knows that if she can pluck the weeds when they're small, just little suspicions, they're easier to nip.

Sometimes it's disconcerting to face all those nasty little negative beliefs, but she says that, disquieting as it is, it's always at least as fascinating as it is uncomfortable.

There are many things you can do to avoid falling into the Polluted Pond. These are three I recommend:

1.     Notice the emotions and feelings you have when you start to think of yourself as "old." Are you sad? Embarrassed? Angry? Resigned? You might even write down your feelings in a notebook, or talk about them with a friend who supports you in staying out of the pond. Whatever the feeling, it probably carries with it a sense of being diminished.

2.   Make a commitment to yourself every morning, that if those feelings come up, you'll do something about them right away. Not "later," or that night, or even on your coffee break. Right away! Otherwise they'll slip away from you, you won't do anything about them, and that will make you feel even more diminished.

You may be able to deal with it immediately, all by yourself, just by saying, "Oh, there it is again. I guess I was starting to fall into the pond, but I'm going to pull myself out again right now." Pull out, examine the thing you were feeling badly about, and see if it's true for you at this time in your life.

It may be something you have to handle with another person. About a month ago, my employee, Ron, and I cleared up a misunderstanding. When we were through, I said to him, "You know, when you repeat things like that, I think you think I can't hear well."

That was the last thing on his mind, of course; it was just one of my own fears. He looked at me as if to say, "What on earth are you talking about?" I don't regret having said it, though. It was very important for me to clear up something that made me uncomfortable, rather than just walking away or trying to hide what I thought was a slight to me because I'm older. That wasn't going on with him at all, of course, but the effect would have been the same for me if I'd just let it go.

If I'd just turned and walked away silently, I would have reinforced within myself the fears that: a) I really was losing my hearing, and b) Ron thought of me as old and "over the hill" for that reason. Instead, I turned what might have been a loss into a huge win for me and for Ron. Ron and I got closer, because I was open with him about my fears. I realized it was just a fear, and not a reality. Everyone benefited, and I felt enhanced rather than diminished.

3.   Take a stand for yourself. Step out, tell the truth about yourself and claim all of who you are, regardless of what people might think.

For years, I was afraid to tell people how much I loved to dance and to gamble, because I was afraid they wouldn't think those were very cultured or intellectual activities. I'd say I just gambled to pass the time waiting for someone else, or I just danced for exercise. The truth is, I'd rather dance than eat, and though I'm not about to lose my mortgage, I love to go to Reno or Tahoe and gamble!

A while back, I decided it was just too much trouble to keep up the smokescreen. I decided that if people couldn't accept me the way I was, then too bad. I stopped hiding my love of dancing and gambling and, to my amazement, people thought it was fantastic! Either that, or they didn't have any interest in it one way or another, and never had. The only difference after I told them was that *I* felt terrific. The more I step out and claim the parts of me I think no one will like, the more fun I have and the more people want to be around me.

### It's Your Life: Payoffs and Choices

Not everybody *wants* to avoid the Polluted Pond. One woman shared with me that if she stopped acting helpless, her children wouldn't call her as often. If she *could* drive, then they wouldn't drive her to the doctor. The payoffs for acting old and helpless were worth more to her than her independence, aliveness, sense of productivity.

We don't have to avoid the pond. It's just a choice, and one that each of us must make for ourselves. Before we can make the choice, we need to know what our particular payoffs might be. Can you think of any ways you actually benefit, overtly or covertly, by being or acting "old?" If so, are they worth it?

Another woman told me she didn't want to take a certain awareness training because she knew she'd find out she really wanted to leave her husband, and she didn't want to disrupt her life. This woman had made a conscious choice, and was very clear about what she didn't want to do. More power to her, because she had looked at all the alternatives and was telling the truth. She preferred the payoff, told the truth about it, and has a better chance of being at peace with herself.

Another woman of forty uses her age as an excuse to eat two hot fudge sundaes every day. "Hey, I'm forty," she says, "You can't expect me to stay trim when I'm getting on in years." Meanwhile, she doesn't really like the way she looks. Unlike the woman who didn't want to leave her husband, she's not at peace with herself. She bought being old as an excuse not to feel alive, vibrant and healthy. The payoff is she has an excuse for being fat, but she's not telling the truth about it. She's not fat because she's forty; she's fat because she eats two hot fudge sundaes every day.

Avoiding the Polluted Pond isn't something you *have* to do; it's just one of several alternatives.

*The Rewards of Not Buying In*

I was brought up not to flatter myself or be conceited, so turning around some of these negative assumptions has been hard for me. I hate to think what would have happened to me if I'd said when I was a child, "I'm terrific! I can have my life be any way I want!" I've had to train myself to be positive about my self-image, but it's been worth it.

The main thing I feel when I find myself not buying into the Polluted Pond, or clearing up something about aging with another person, or generally taking a stand for myself, is ELATION. It's almost a physical feeling, coursing through my whole body, and it seems to affect everyone around me. They feel better, too. It's such an exquisite pleasure that it takes me not just from 0 to $+10$, but from $-10$ to $+20$!

It's the difference between approaching life from a position of being afraid people will find out something about me, and knowing I can be all of myself and make my life as full and creative as I want. It's fear about surviving from one day to the next vs. the joy of creating life.

*SECRET #2*: DON'T BUY INTO THE POLLUTED POND.

Examine each issue separately, and don't buy the whole pond if it isn't true for you. Realize that you're in charge of whether you buy in or not. Check out the payoffs and make that choice.

4.
## WHERE THE POLLUTED POND COMES FROM AND HOW IT WORKS

*How It Begins*

The Polluted Pond is everywhere in our society—in advertising magazines, movies, TV, the fashion and beauty industries, just about anywhere you look. We're reminded of it constantly when we interact with parents, children, peers, business associates and friends. Someone says or does something that triggers our insecurities, and immediately we're tempted to fall in.

The pond is hard to avoid. We just have to remember that nothing and no one outside of ourselves has anything to do with whether or not we fall in.

The Polluted Pond doesn't just descend of us, full-blown. It takes years for us to get into a position where we're receptive to it, and that training begins at a very early age. It starts the very first time we get the notion that we're not all right the way we are.

All of us have a first experience of something being wrong with us. That time when we first realize we weren't all right just the way we were. It could have been a well-meaning aunt who made an offhand comment. "My, what big ears she has." It could have been a hairstylist who said, "Well, she'll always have to deal with that double chin," or friends at school who teased us about being taller than all the boys.

At first, it's hard to remember what that experience was. If we could remember it right away, it would be on the conscious level and we could look at it, deal with it, and get rid of it. We could see that it never was true, or that it's no longer true, and we'd be in great shape. Usually, though, we have to dig a little to get to it.

The most common experience people have when they find those first incidents is that the thing they were so worried about isn't even true—or it was true at one time, but isn't any longer.

A girl might have been 5'7" in seventh grade, and felt weird and not okay because she was taller than the rest of the kids. Now she's forty years old, still 5'7", and about average height. The only thing is, she still feels weird.

Another woman may have been told at the age of ten that she couldn't wear bangs, so she's never worn them. Now she's thirty, and has an entirely different face. Even in the unlikely event that what she heard back then was an informed, expert opinion, it has no validity now. And it may *never* have been true.

You don't have to carry around those beliefs forever. Check them out now, with yourself or with someone else who knows what they're doing.

I can't tell you how many people sit down in my chair and say things like, "Well, of course I should never wear my hair shorter than my ears." I look at them and can't imagine where

27

they got that idea. Maybe they read it in a magazine. Maybe some stylist in Moline, Illinois, told them that when they went to their granduncle's funeral. Maybe they had a favorite movie star who never wore her hair shorter than her ears. Who knows? The trouble is, if we're not sure ourselves, we assume that someone else—anyone else—knows better than we do.

If someone comes in mortified about her "large forehead" and tries to work her whole hairstyle around that, I might say very casually, "Who told you about your large forehead?" The client answers, "Oh, you know, my grandmother always used to say I did." Her grandmother? What is she, the editor of *Vogue*?

So I say, "Well, let's take a look at it now and see if it's still true today." Nine out of ten times it isn't and that woman sees herself as if for the first time, through entirely new eyes. She's let go of the filter that says, "Now I have to look at myself in the mirror, but I know I'm going to have a large forehead." Until she lets go of that filter, there is no hairstyle on earth that's going to make her happy or make her forehead look any smaller to her.

### Negative Decisions

Usually, the insecurities and negative beliefs stem from passing comments, uninformed opinions, and vague notions we've gathered from people who, for the most part, have no idea what they're talking about. Nevertheless, we buy it and can let it run our lives.

I sometimes have people make a list of ten beliefs they have about the way they look, and then ask them to examine each belief from the perspective of how they look now, as opposed to how they looked when they formed the opinion. In most cases, only about two of those ideas have anything to do with the present situation.

The foundation for the Polluted Pond gets laid very early, and usually there's one big thing about us that's not okay. For me, it was my thighs. I always thought they were too big, even though I was always fairly slim. Whenever people would compliment me I'd think (and sometimes say), "Yeah, but you don't know about my thighs. It's a good thing I'm wearing this full skirt so you can't find out the worst about me."

Here's an exercise I suggest to people who want to work on

28

getting rid of those negative decisions. I call it the Mirror Exercise. Stand in front of a mirror and look at yourself, but not the way you've ever looked at yourself before. Start at the top of your head and work your way down to your toes, noticing all the negative decisions that come up. You don't have to start believing them all over again, just notice they're there. See if they have any validity now. It's not likely that they do.

Then go back and look at yourself through new eyes, as if you'd never made those decisions. You may even want to make a positive affirmation that's different from the decision, and start changing the pattern of your thinking.

### How It Grows

As the years pass, one decision leads to another. They build, one on top of the other, until they form a firm, solid foundation of negative thinking and a point of view that "I'm not okay the way I am."

First it was the large forehead, so we start out from the point of view that we're not all right. Then maybe we start thinking, or someone tells us, or we decide after reading a magazine, that our eyes are too close together. The negative beliefs are getting deeper, firmer. Then maybe we gain five pounds. At this point, it's going to be hard to do *anything* right.

Then one day, we see something negative that also looks *old*. A grey hair, sagging skin, lines around the eyes, something that says we're not what we used to be or what we want to be. The stage is set. By now, it's easy to be negative. What's the natural thing to do? Right. Fall right into the Polluted Pond.

The pond is a whole new level of negativity. Everyone agrees about it, so no one's going to argue with you if you decide to jump in. You *are* getting older. The pond is huge, and so accessible! Everybody *else* is doing it. If you ever had any thought that you might like to give up and just not try anymore, here is your excuse. You could jump into that pond, wrap it around you forever, and never again have to be accountable for anything. How *could* you do any more, be anymore than you are? You're *old*!

### How To Crack It

Surprisingly enough, there is a fairly simple way out of this morass. I've seen people discover that they've fallen into the pond, and then decide they don't want to be there anymore. They start by going back and trying to find that first, original negative decision they made about themselves. That's their key to unraveling the knot and letting themselves out of the trap.

They look for that first incident, that first time they began thinking they weren't okay. The dig around in their memory for the decision that opened the door for all the others, the one on which the others are based. The amazing thing is that, if they can get to that original decision, if they can feel or remember when they made it and why, then very often the entire foundation of negativity crumbles and falls away. They look at themselves freshly and clearly for the first time in decades, without the filter of all that negativity.

That doesn't mean that they become perfect overnight, or that they never think another negative thought. It just means they start appreciating themselves a little, and start looking at themselves in terms of their own natural resonance and perfection, rather than looking for flaws and imperfections and beating themselves to a pulp about it.

I do classes for teens, and sometimes I run across girls who say, "Well, I don't really like my mouth much, but I like myself so that's okay." There may be some things about themselves they'd like to change, but that doesn't mean they have to be completely negative about themselves. You don't have to believe, overnight, that you are the most gorgeous thing in the world, but starting to chip away at those negative beliefs begins a whole new pattern of relating to yourself and enjoying your life.

The First Decision Exercise can be very helpful in getting to those early decision. Choose a quiet time when you won't be disturbed, and try to recall the first negative decision you ever made about yourself. It probably happened when you were quite young, so you may have to go back in time. What was that decision? How old were you? How did you carry it forward into your life? Can you let go of it?

*It Can Start At Any Age*
1.   Pre-teens. Believe it or not, there are pre-teens who worry about aging. To most people, aging means lost opportunities, and we can believe that we've lost opportunities...or are about to lose them...at any age. A boy of ten may feel old when he

gets a new brother or sister and realizes he'll never really be his mom's baby again, or when his family moves and he has to leave all his pals, or when he gets too old to be a Cub Scout.

2.  Teens. People also see aging in terms of achievement and productivity. "What have I accomplished? Is it too late to go back to school, start a new job?" Some people see aging as an end to potential. To a teen, aging might mean missing the chance to go to the prom, to college, an end to being in school. It might mean never being financially dependent again. (That'll start the grey hairs popping!)

3.  Twenties. In their twenties, people sometimes start feeling old if they haven't found a mate, or if they're not dating. This may also be a time when they see the first extra pounds or wrinkles. I've known twenty-five-year-old women who considered themselves over the hill and gave up on being attractive and getting married just because they looked in the mirror and didn't see what they thought they should. They hadn't fulfilled all those romantic childhood fantasies, so they thought they had failed.

A twenty-seven-year-old client named Gail told me she'd been living with her boyfriend for two years and had felt great about it until her grandmother came to town and started giving her a hard time about being "twenty-seven and not married!" Now Gail says that's all she can think about. She feels like she's getting older by the minute, should have gotten married years ago, is running out of time, and has done everything wrong.

4.  Thirties. Let's take a woman through each decade, and see which fears come up. The thirties get a little more complicated. She may be married now, but it might not be quite as romantic as she thought it would be. She has a couple kids, a lot of bills, and a husband who's spending more and more time at the office. She feels a little dull, tied down, and constricted. She has almost no time for herself. (In my thirties, raising four children, I considered myself lucky if I got a bath every day!) When she does look in the mirror, she's shocked at what she sees, and starts making wholesale decisions about how old and frumpy she is.

It's just as scary for her unmarried counterpart, who is even *more* single in her thirties than she was in her twenties. She feels like a biological time bomb about having kids, doesn't really know if she wants to give up her independence, but sort of thinks there must be something wrong with her if she doesn't have a family. When this woman starts seeing grey hair, everything is multiplied by five.

And by now, it's very likely she *is* seeing some grey hair, or some other signs of physical aging. Not only that, but she starts to talk about it with her friends, who are experiencing the same thing. Double trouble. Now the aging process is not only visual, it's beginning to get cemented into place with conversation.

5.  Forties. The forties may be the most difficult decade. If the woman has children, they're likely to be in their teens when she is in her forties. Teenagers are wonderful, and we all had to go through that stage, but I'd be hard pressed to say they are the most secure or considerate people in the world, or that their parents are their favorite people during those uncomfortable years.

Teens are apt to make insensitive, hurtful comments that reflect their parent's age. Unless you realize they're just talking about their own insecurities, and don't let their words trigger *your* insecurities, it can be very, very hard.

In addition, when you have kids who are teens, it becomes very clear not only that you are no longer the younger generation, but that you *never will be again.*

And what happens to kids after they're teenagers? They leave home! Now the whole household is different, and the woman's focus is different. She looks across the living room and sees George. For the past twenty years, she's been relating to him mostly through the kids. Do they have anything to say to each other now? Does he still find her attractive? Even though she may be starting to go through the *menopause!* And that in itself is difficult. To make matters worse, her husband now looks better than ever. He's really coming into his own professionally, and is looking more gorgeous by the day.

Anyone who makes it through their forties without falling into the Polluted Pond should have it made, but sometimes it doesn't work out that way.

6.  Fifties. In the fifties, the kids have probably left home for good. The woman has devoted her whole life to this family, and now they're gone. She realizes that she's not really kept up her appearance, her reading, her more exciting friendships, her interest in the outside world, and she starts to wonder where she's been for the past thirty years. Where does she belong now?

Who is she and where is her place? *Is* there a place for her?

7.  Sixties. In the sixties, she gets to be a grandparent—for some people, the very definition of being old. My own mother would never let herself be called "grandma" for just that reason. This is a milestone. We bought into the whole story about grandparents even before we were ten. Now we're talking about serious "old."

We're talking retirement, possible diminishment of hearing and sight, pensions, Social Security, and a whole raft of things that our society associates with being old. It gets easier and easier to buy in, and there are more and more people who'll agree that it's all true—we're near the end, it's just a matter of hanging on as best we can and trying not to be so much of a burden, a question of trying to make the money last as long as we can.

Children start asking, "And you sure you should be alone at night?" They call to make sure the doors are locked.

I know one woman who didn't fall into this trap. She was so unwilling to think of herself as an "old woman" that she deliberately went out and spent her Social Security payments on jewelry. Not everyone can afford to do that, and most of us would consider it a bit extravagant, but it was her way of saying that she didn't have to throw in the towel, that she was just as capable in her sixties as she had been in her forties and fifties.

8.  Seventies, Eighties and Beyond. The seventies and eighties often bring more of the same, except that sometimes there are the added elements of regret and blame—regret at the missed opportunities (now is when people wish they were sixty again), and blaming others for what's wrong in the world and in their own lives. Accidents and injuries get more frequent, especially if that's what people expect will happen.

Do all these grim things have to happen? Absolutely not!

*What You Can Do*

1.  *Do what you want, not what you should.* You don't have to live a certain way just because other people expect you to. Set your own standards and goals. Don't live your life wondering what other people will think.

You don't have to have a lot of money to do what you want. In fact, sometimes it's more fun to go to the library than to do something glamorous. After my kids left home and I had a little nestegg, I decided the thing I should do was go to Europe. I saw and did all the traditional things, but I discovered I didn't really enjoy traveling like that.

I hated living out of a suitcase and running for planes, and realized that, although I'd enjoyed seeing all the treasures of art and culture, I'd gone to Europe the way I *thought* people should go to Europe, rather than looking at what I wanted.

I saw that what I really wanted to do was go to one place and *move in* for three to six months. A year ago, when I was fifty-nine, I decided to stay in Rappalo, Italy, for six months. I didn't know anyone there, and didn't speak Italian, but I wanted to find out more about who I was and see if I could survive without my props around me—my salon, family, friends, clients, employees, etc. It was a big risk, and there were times when I was very uncomfortable, but it was also a tremendous experience. I grew by leaps and bounds, and traveled in a way that was right for *me*.

2. *Be yourself.* The reason some people are reluctant to be themselves is that they're afraid of *being found out*. I see very nice, upstanding people—especially women—walking around the streets like criminals. Their posture, the expressions on their faces, they way they relate to others, all suggest they think there's some terrible, secret inadequacy deep within them, and that the main thing they're trying to do in life is keep people from finding out.

3. *Break the mold. Don't let age determine your interests or activities.* In each decade, people will have certain ideas about what you should be doing or not doing. Remember that those are their ideas, not yours. They don't necessarily coincide with what you want.

Forget what you *should* be doing in each decade. You may want to sit home with a book all through your twenties and date up a storm when you're in your eighties. So what if people think you should slave away with your house and kids in your thirties? Hire a babysitter, or trade with a friend, and take the afternoon off if you want to give yourself some attention.

In the forties, you can remember that your kids' teen years are even harder for them than they are for you, and they're going to take some of it out on you just because you're closest to them. They don't always mean to hurt you, and even when they do it's just because they feel so insecure themselves. Don't let *their* insecurities trigger *yours*. Just stay calm, don't stop trusting that you are a good and valuable person, and remember that this, too, shall pass.

4.  *Choose your friends and activities carefully.* When a woman's children leave home, it's almost as if she's starting from scratch. She has to create a whole new life for herself.

While the kids were growing up, all she could think about was the freedom she'd have when they were grown, the luxurious bubble baths she'd take, the afternoons of shopping, the candlelight dinners with her husband. Then when they actually do leave, it's quite a shock. Her first reaction may be, "Oh my God, what do I do now?"

My friend Mary found herself in this situation. She tried going back to the kinds of activities and friends she'd had before the kids, and it proved disastrous. Twenty years had passed. She wasn't the same person, and she wasn't living in the same world. She wasn't satisfied with the same people and things that had satisfied her when she was younger.

Mary discovered that a lot of her old friends and activities weren't stimulating anymore, and became very selective about the people she saw and how she spent her time. She didn't like sitting around all the time gossiping with Mildred about Sarah, who never gets anything done around her house, or about the kids, who will never learn. It just wasn't fun or exciting, and seemed to perpetuate the same old negative situations. She always felt tired or vaguely uncomfortable when she left.

Nor did she like spending a lot of time with people who challenged everything she said or did, or who didn't seem to want *her* to grow or change. She got suspicious of people who always questioned, "Gee, are you sure that's a good idea? It's pretty risky, isn't it?"

Mary didn't want to be snobbish, but neither did she want to be bogged down, unsupported or bored. She realized that people grow in different directions, and even good friends don't have to be lifelong friends or see one another every day.

Mary hasn't given up all her friends or family. She will always have certain people in her life, but there are other people whom she doesn't see as often as she used to. They know Mary will always be there for them, and that they can always call on her, but she doesn't call them up every time she has a free hour.

35

I've experienced some of the same things Mary has. When I have free time, I ask myself first what I want to do. Then I ask myself if I want to do it alone or with someone else. Then I ask myself with whom I want to do it. It might be an old friend, or I might call someone interesting whom I met last week. Again, it gets back to making choices. Continually making choices is less comfortable than doing the same thing over and over without examining it, but those choices make life a lot more interesting.

There are many, many more things you can do to avoid falling into the Polluted Pond, and some of them are covered in Chapter Eight. For now, you'll be ahead of the game if you can just remember to stay in the here and now, to be yourself and appreciate yourself just the way you are, to do what you want rather than what you should, and to choose your friends and activities carefully.

You are the only one who can make your life positive.

*SECRET #3*: CONCENTRATE ON YOUR NATURAL PERFECTION, RESONANCE AND HARMONY RATHER THAN ON FAULTS OR IMPERFECTIONS.

Look at yourself with a new focus. We're all raised to be humble and not to "compliment ourselves," but that can turn into a deadly trap of self-criticism and beating ourselves up, and vastly reduce our enjoyment of life. We don't have to be what our parents called "conceited," but I think it's a shame not to enjoy the perfection and beauty we were given as part of nature.

## 5.
## WHY WE FALL IN

*Who Leads Us Astray?*

Obviously, no one can really lead us astray but ourselves. No one can push us into the Polluted Pond; we have to jump. There are, however, some outside influences that can be pretty strong. They begin early in life and go right through to the end, providing us with exciting challenges every step of the way. A few of these influences are:

1. *Parents:* We don't usually think of parents pushing their children into the Polluted Pond. It seems like such an awful

thing to do, and besides, it's hard to imagine children being concerned with age. We forget that concern with aging is, first and foremost, a concern with *not being okay*. This, at least, is where it begins.

Have you ever seen a mother and daughter shopping together, and thought that one of them was about to pull a weapon from her purse? The mother grabs skirts from the rack, exclaiming about how pretty they are, and how they're going to make the daughter look much better than the ragged jeans she's wearing, especially if she'd only stand up straight.

The daughter sulks in the corner, trying to disappear into the racks of clothes, rolling her eyes and casting murderous glances at her mother. This doesn't make her any more attractive, so the mother tries harder. She's more determined than ever that her daughter will *have fun* and *be pretty*—just like she was, or wishes she had been.

This, of course, is the problem. Parents want the best for their children, which is why they're always after them to "be better." That's fine, but parents' intentions aren't always so altruistic. It's also natural for parents to try to live out their own fantasies, or relive their own pasts, through their children. This makes kids absolutely nuts.

The kids feel awkward and inadequate enough to begin with, especially as teens, and when they sense the added burden of having to live up to their parents' own standards for themselves— many of which are based on ideas and images that are thirty or forty years old—it's just too much. They close down, stop communicating, and withdraw into their shells, which makes the parents even more anxious.

Remember, the things we resist are the things that persist. With this mother and daughter, there's a double resistance. It's a push-pull, back and forth battle that keeps everybody stuck right where they are. Who is going to back down? They both think they're doing the right thing.

The mother wants her child to be gorgeous, responsible, secure, brilliant and perfect—all the things she wants or wanted to be and isn't. If the child doesn't measure up, the mother somehow blames herself. But how is she going to teach her daughter to do something she still doesn't understand how to do herself? The child gets defensive and confused, doesn't know exactly what is expected of her, and wouldn't want to knuckle under even if she did.

The mother presses all the time, trying to make up for having done it wrong *last* time, talking either directly to her daughter or, worse, to someone else *about* her. "Sally just won't spend the time to put herself together nicely." "Sally doesn't know how to wear makeup right, but I tell her..."

Sally is screaming, figuratively or literally, "GET OFF MY BACK!" Not only has her mother made it almost impossible for her to move and change, but she's gotten across the message loud and clear that Sally is *not all right the way she is.*

The irony is that kids usually want nothing more than to change, to grow, to move and get better. All of us do. It's part of being human. The main thing that keeps kids stuck is their parents' resistance. If they were left alone, they'd move so quickly they'd be practically unrecognizable in a week. But they can't and won't be pushed. The only way to get them to move is to allow them to be where they are, which is the last thing parents want to do.

It's painful for parents, because they only want the best for their kids. It's hard to see them move through phases that are uncomfortable, and even unattractive. It requires a real leap of faith to trust that they'll move through all the right places for them and come out where they're supposed to be—especially if their first instinct is to wear a plastic trash bags and purple spiked hair. Parents need to remember that, next week, it'll be button down shirts and gabardine slacks.

Here are a few facts that can make it easier to let go, and allow kids to be where they are:

1. Trying to make them move absolutely doesn't work. In fact, it produces the opposite result and keeps them stuck.

2. Trying to make them move gives them the message: "You are not all right the way you are, and have to change in order to be acceptable."

3. Communication breaks down when kids feel pressured. They can't figure out a way to win, other than to knuckle under. They clam up and withdraw into their shells, and this affects all other aspects of the relationship.

4. In the end, trying to force them to move is just more trouble than it's worth. It doesn't get parents what they want,

and sets up other negative situations for the child and for the relationship between parent and child.

It would be wonderful if parents could just let their children be. But then, it would be wonderful if everyone on earth could just let everyone else be. Since that's not the case just yet, the best we can do is recognize the temptation, understand that it's motivated by the best of intentions, and do the best we can.

2.   *Children:* We've talked about how children in their teens can be difficult for parents who are already hovering near the edges of the pond. It can start even earlier. One of my daughters once asked me if I remembered much about the covered wagons. I'm sixty years old and have grey hair, but that seemed a little extreme.

Kids sometimes don't have any sense of time or history, and are likely to ask what it was like before electricity or the steam engine. With technology moving as fast as it is, this problem may get even worse. I know parents in their thirties who feel ancient watching their children play with computers.

Having kids is always going to make you feel a little older. It becomes strikingly clear, every day, that you are no longer part of the younger generation. The trick is not to let "being older" become part of your bottom-line thinking. It's a real challenge to stay centered in the midst of this hurricane.

Not having children can also create concern about aging. My friend Alice, who is thirty-nine, was shopping with her friend. The friend commented on Alice's flat stomach, then sort of looking up at the ceiling and said, "Of course, you've never had children." As if, "You'd *better* have a flat stomach. You don't have any excuses!" If you don't have children in this society, you'd better have and do a *lot* of things. You'd better set higher standard of appearance and achievement, and you'd better meet them.

3.   *Peers:* Peer pressure starts very early, rises dramatically in the teens, and continues as long as we let it.

For teens, it's usually a question of feeling so insecure about who they are and how they look that they don't dare do, say, or wear anything different from the rest of the crowd. If the other kids are wearing a particular kind of blouse or a particular hairstyle, some teens will do *anything* to get it. No one wants to be "out of it," left behind, or not part of the group. Not all teens

e this, of course. I love seeing kids who don't succumb to
nd of pressure, but they are rare.

As we get older and move into our thirties, peer pressure
almost becomes a competition. Who has the nicest house, the
best-behaved kids, the richest husband? Who has managed to
keep herself up a little more than the others?

What if you don't come out on top? This is when it's easiest
to fall into the pond. What if things haven't turned out exactly
the way you thought they would, or hoped they would? Do you
throw in the towel, give up on possibilities, say you're getting
older and are more tired anyway, so who cares? Only if that's
what you really want.

Again, the solution is simply to recognize that the problem
exists, and know that you don't have to fall into it. At any
moment in our lives, we can start over, begin fresh, and create
a life that's exciting and full.

The Party Exercise can give clues to what you think other
people think of you. *Imagine* that you're at a party where you
don't know anyone. Suddenly, across the room, you see two
people you know. They're talking to one another, and you start
moving toward them. As you come close, you hear your name.
They're talking about you. What are they saying? How do you
react?

Don't necessarily *believe* everything you hear. Just remember
that what you believe others think of you can affect how you
approach life—if you let it.

4.  *Society:* No one needs to be told about the ways in which
our society has been prejudiced against older people. We've seen
it in advertising, movies, TV, and any number of other places.
As the median age of people (and consumers) in America gets
higher, we're seeing less and less of this kind of prejudice, but
some of it remains.

That doesn't mean, however, that we have to succumb to the
idea that older people are less valuable or able. We don't have
to think the way the media wants us to think. We're in charge
of our own thoughts, and our own lives.

5.  *Ourselves:* We are the only ones who really matter when
it comes to choosing whether or not to fall into the pond. If we
let ourselves, we will. If we don't let ourselves, we won't.

The most common way we trap ourselves is by not staying

current with the way the world is now, and the way we ourselves are now. We start to feel dated, sound dated, look dated, and be dated.

Sometimes that's because we don't know how to be current without looking like we're trying to be younger than we are. A lot of women say this is why they still dress pretty much the way they did ten years ago. They just don't feel comfortable in anything else. When they think about changing, and look in a magazine to see what's new, they see punk rock, mini-skirts, and a lot of things that really *might* make them look ridiculous. They can't make a choice, so they give up altogether.

They forget that there are ways to be current, classic and fashionable without wearing chains, metallic stockings or day-glo tube tops—and that it doesn't have to cost a lot of money.

Sometimes women get stuck in time because they're clinging to a period that was particularly good for them. It may have been when they were in high school, or college, or at some time later in life when they felt they were on top of the world. All the good memories stick with them. That was when they felt great, when the world was full of possibilities, when they were queen of the hop.

That was when they wore the bouffant hairdo, or had their hair in frizzies, or swept around in the Veronica Lake pageboy, or wore the bright red lipstick. Whatever it was, it worked then and it should work now, right? Wrong. The statement it makes is that, back then, these women thought they were making it—and now they don't.

I'm not talking just about clothing, hairstyle and makeup, but also about ways of acting and thinking. The Doris Day and Sophia Loren images don't quite cut it today the way they did in the Fifties and early Sixties. Talking about the good old days doesn't make it, either. I don't want to say that they *weren't* the good old days, or that there isn't richness or value in the past. I just mean that, by living in the past to the exclusion of the present, we cut ourselves off and limit ourselves. And those two things lead directly to the Polluted Pond.

*Why Some People Give Up*

A wonderful bookkeeper named Janet once worked for me. She was just fabulous, but one day about a year after I hired her,

41

she walked up to me and said, "You know I really need to quit, because I'm sixty-two."

"Sixty-two?" I said, "What does that have to do with anything?"

"Well, I should start taking it easy," she replied.

This woman was in great health and thoroughly enjoyed working with us. There was no reason in the world for her to retire, except that she thought that's what she ought to do when she got to be sixty-two.

Janet seemed to give up just because she expected that's what she should do. Other people give up because, for whatever reasons, they want to hide. Sinking beneath the surface of the pond is a great place to hide. These are the people who approach life from, "What can I do to avoid the bad stuff and not get found out?" rather than from the point of view, "What can I do to make my life even better, to know and enjoy myself even more?"

In a way, we all face the choice between these two points of view when we're confronted with the Polluted Pond.

Sometimes it's just easier to give in to all those negative beliefs than to be responsible for creating our own lives and our own reality. Then we can never be blamed if things don't turn out so well, because there was nothing we could have done about it.

The only trouble is that giving up usually ends in sadness, in feelings of not being competent or attractive, in a sense that opportunities are closing quickly and there's very little time left.

The alternative is a little more challenging, and certainly more risky. If we live our lives as if we were really in charge, we're apt to stumble and fall. That's part of the game, though. We all stumble and fall occasionally when we step out and say, "This is my life. I'm in charge and I'm going to make it the best I can." It can be scarey to take that kind of stand, but it's also exhilarating and, in the end, the only way to really live fully.

### Reasons or Results

I knew a woman who always said, "We have our choice in life. We can have the results we want, or we can have the reasons why we don't have them." When I first heard that, I thought, "What a tough cookie. I bet she's never run into the kind of trouble *I* have!" Well, over the years I watched her run into a lot worse trouble than I ever had, and she never wavered. She stuck to that philosophy, and she got a lot more results than she got reasons.

Again, it's all about choice. There are a million reasons to fall into the pond, and no one will ever blame you if you do. They may, in fact, be delighted to have you in the pond with them so they don't have to compete with you. You can all be old and miserable together. But for every reason, there is a way out. There are also a million ways to *keep* from falling into the pond, and the first is to remember who's in charge of whether or not you jump.

I use the Park Bench Exercise to get an idea of how I'm looking at myself and holding my life. Pretend you're sitting on a park bench. You look across the way, see a person sitting on the opposite bench, and that person is you.

What does that person look like? What does she seem to be like? What presence does she project? Is she happy? What does she represent to you?

When you're finished, let go of all your thoughts and images. The purpose of this exercise is not to see yourself as particularly positive or negative, but simply to be objective and see how you *do* see yourself, so that you can go on and create a new reality if you wish...or simply appreciate the old one more.

*SECRET #4*: REMEMBER THAT YOU'RE IN CHARGE.

Your attitudes shape your age and your level of aliveness, the amount of joy and grace and find in living. You're holding the reins. It's your life, and you can do absolutely anything you want with it. No one, no matter how strong their influence, can push you into the pond—and only you can jump. You may want to do that, but remember it's your choice.

# 6.
# AGE AND BEAUTY

*What Is Beautiful?*

Beauty doesn't have to mean anything physical. It doesn't mean long or short hair, dark or blonde hair, voluptuous or skinny bodies, blue or brown eyes. It doesn't mean any of the combinations of physical traits that have, at various times, been on the covers of magazines.

To me, beauty is a sense of inner harmony and resonance with oneself that reflects outward into our physical appearance. It doesn't mean perfect features, peaches and cream skin, or any of the other "ideals" we sometimes think we need to be attractive.

It's simply a sense of wholeness, of self-acceptance and going out to others, of saying, "I care about myself and those around me enough to give myself some attention, to present my own 'natural beauty in the best way I can."

This person pays attention to the way nature has put the colors together in her hair, skin and eyes, and choses clothing that reflects and enhances that natural resonance. She chooses lines that feel right on her and follow the flow of her body and her inner essence. She can look herself in the eye in the mirror and like what she sees.

I'm not talking about the person who spends three hours putting herself together because she's afraid people will find out what she *really* looks like. That woman is functioning out of fear and survival, not coming into the world joyfully and creatively.

I'm talking about the person who has taken the time, and had the courage, to look in the mirror and see herself as the people who love her would see her. She sees herself as part of nature's perfection, appreciates herself as she was meant to be appreciated, and holds herself this way in front of others, rather than retreating back into the mud of self-criticism and false humility.

It's difficult and frustrating to deal with a person who won't let you compliment her. You say, "What a great coat!" She says, "This old thing? Oh, I got it for a quarter at a garage sale and only wear it when my other one's at the cleaners." How does that make you feel?

Sometimes people act as if they'll be punished if they accept a compliment, and perhaps they have been. They'll be considered "conceited" and "selfish·"

"You look great today, Betty," you say.

"Oh, with these bags under my eyes? I didn't sleep all night because..." Then they're off on some entirely different subject. Or, "Oh, I gained five pounds last week. How can you say that?" Or, "This hair is making me crazy, it's so..." No matter what the response, it's something negative about themselves, and it makes you feel uncomfortable. Do these kinds of responses make you think any more of the person, or make her any more attractive to you? Of course not.

The person I consider beautiful isn't conceited." She doesn't sit back eating bonbons and smugly accepting compliments all day. She doesn't really need compliments because she feels so good about herself, but she does accept them graciously when they come along.

When I see people like this, I get a sense of peace. I see that it's possible to have that kind of relationship with oneself, and I see how special it is. That's inspiring.

Sometimes I ask people to do an exercise called Your Ideal Self, in which they sit back and envision themselves just the way they would like to be—not necessarily physically, but emotionally, mentally, spiritually. Then I ask them to write down a description of the Ideal Self who comes up, and what she would do in the following situations.

What kind of work does she do and how does she relate to it? How does she interact with the people at work? What is she like with her friends? How does she respond to various situations with them? How does she relate to her family? Are they close? Communicative? Affectionate? Strict? What kinds of activities does she pursue? What kinds of things does she think and say? What is in the inner essence she puts out into the world?

At first, people are inclined to say, "Oh, I could never be like that!" The amazing thing is that, if they do this with any conviction or regularity, they start actually becoming the people they want to be. The ideal becomes the real. I think this kind of exercise becomes more and more important as we grow older. We not only start creating our own reality, but we see again that beauty isn't entirely a function of our physical selves.

You don't have to look like someone on the cover of a magazine in order to be beautiful. In this chapter, we'll explore the special ways you can actually become more beautiful as you grow older. We'll talk about what happens with makeup, hair coloring and going to the beauty salon as you get older. Then we'll look at the Number One Pitfall that makes people look older than they are, and how to avoid it so you can look your very best at any age.

### Makeup

Makeup can be tremendously enhancing, but you have to feel good about wearing it before it can start working for you. If you feel silly, or don't think you've done it right, it's probably better

45

not to wear much—or to find out what you need to know in order for it to feel good.

If you *feel* like you look like a clown, whether you do or not, the makeup won't do anything for you except create what they call in Star Wars, "a tremor in the force." People will sense that you feel funny, and start feeling that way themselves, even if they don't know exactly what the problem is.

If you don't feel like you know enough about makeup to do it in a way that feels good to you, get some help from a professional. Don't hope, or pray, or use guesswork. Find out what you need to know from a pro who can give advice about your particular skin and coloring. Most salons have makeup specialist. If yours doesn't, another one in your area probably does. If you only have a little money to spend on makeup, this is the place to spend it. When you know what you're doing, you don't waste money on things you don't use or that aren't flattering to you.

Makeup is very individual, both in terms of color and contour, and we won't attempt to do a hundred faces here just to give you a general idea of what may or may not work for you. There are, however, some basic fashion trends you can use as guidelines. As you learn more about your own colors and design lines (which we'll discuss in a later chapter), you'll be able to blend your own style with fashion trends so that you look current without losing your individual flair.

I can't stress enough the important of foundations—for women of any age. Foundations do three very important things:
1.   They seal in the skin's natural moisture.
2.   They protect your face from the environment by keeping out dirt and pollutants.
3.   They smooth out irregular blotches and redness.

All these things are very important, especially as your skin grows older. I'm not saying everyone should wear foundation all the time; I'm just suggesting that you not exclude the possibility. Not only will foundations protect your skin, but they can be tremendously enhancing. The don't have to be the pastey, stage-makeup goos we sometimes associate with the word "foundation."

*Skin Care*

Europeans are far ahead of us when it comes to appreciating the importance of skin care. Mothers send their daughters to learn about skin care as soon as they're in their teens, which is when serious skin care should begin.

The best way to approach skin care is to have your skin analyzed by an expert, and get his or her advice. These are some general principles:

AT NIGHT:

1. Never, ever go to bed with makeup on. Be sure you give your skin a thorough cleaning every night.

2. Tonics, lotions and astringents act as balancers to the skin after cleansing, and also remove any extra grime that cleansing leaves behind.

3. Next, use a moisturizer and the right night cream—with additives if your skin needs them.

IN THE MORNING:

1. Cleanse your skin again. This is important. You'd be surprised how dirty it can get during the night.

2. Use a light tonic or astringent.

3. Moisturize your skin again. Always wear moisturizer under your makeup, and of course moisturize even if you don't use makeup.

Facials and masks you can do at home are important parts of skin care, too. Both remove dead skin cells and leave the skin looking and feeling fresh, as well as helping prevent wrinkles. Different types of skin demand different types of masks, however. Ask your expert which ones are best for you.

Water, water everywhere. Drinking water is one of the very best things you can do for your skin. When I see a woman with beautiful skin, I always ask her what her secret is. More often than not, she tells me she drinks eight glasses of water a day. Water keeps your skin glowing with moisture year after year.

They say smoking causes wrinkles, so if you're serious about skin care I'd stay away from cigarettes. And never, never squeeze blemishes.

The face is our most important area. It always shows, and we don't pay nearly enough attention to taking care of it. Take some time to be kind to your face and give it some special care.

*Hair Coloring*

People start coloring their hair for any number of reasons that have nothing at all to do with grey hair and, quite often, nothing to do with choice. Later, when they haven't seen their real color for ten, twenty, or thirty years, the issue of hair coloring gets mixed up with the issue of grey hair. They don't know exactly what's underneath the tint, but they're pretty sure it's a lot of grey so they don't dare stop. Wherever the notion that grey hair was bad came from, they've bought into it.

We have an entire chapter on Grey Hair, and we'll talk at length about coloring to cover grey (or NOT coloring to cover grey) in that chapter. Here, we'll just talk about the general issue of coloring your hair, and the choices that are available to you.

After forty years of experience, I recommend that people think long and hard about coloring their hair. There are many, many reasons never to start coloring your hair. Among them are:

1.   Your own color is there for a reason, and works in harmony and resonance with the colors of yours eyes and skin. In most cases, finding these resonances and working with them gives you much more of a "pick-me-up" than you could ever get by coloring your hair. If you must tint, choose a color that's as close as possible to your own. The farther away you get from your own color, the more you increase the risk of getting into real trouble with the color you select.

2.   Once you start coloring your hair, it can get to be a habit. If you ever want to stop, there's a long, awkward process, and you're stuck with a lifetime of coloring your hair. It becomes a habit that you never really chose, all for a color that probably wasn't chosen correctly, doesn't suit your skin tones, and probably never did.

3.   It's expensive.

4.   It's time-consuming.

5.   You can become a slave to your cycle of hair coloring. The party is always the day *before* you have your appointment, and then nothing happens for three weeks. If you go out of town on a long trip, you either take your chances with getting your hair colored on the road, or you live with roots. (Very few people carry the right formula for their color along with them, or can find someone to duplicate it exactly even if they did.) You can only count on looking good—or at least getting *done*—as long as you're close to your hairstylist.

*How and Why I stopped*

I used to color my hair all the time. I did it for twenty years, starting when I was in beauty college. That's what you did when you were in beauty college; you colored your hair. Everybody did it. Every three weeks, when we got our hair tinted or bleached, we'd try a new color. It was like trying out recipes from a magazine. I did it all through the Fifties and Sixties.

Then I had my colors done by a color analyst. This woman looked at the color of my eyes, skin, and what she could find of my real hair. She chose a set of colors for me that would draw out my own natural combinations, and gave me swatches. I could then take these colors with me when I went shopping for clothes or even for furnishings for my home. This woman was always suggesting that if I had to tint my hair, I should go for this one particular shade of light, ashy, greyish brown.

Well, I never had any idea what the hair coloring would actually look like on my hair, even when I saw a sample. It was Russian roulette to see how it was going to combine with what was already on my hair, how much my hair had been out in the sun, what my body chemistry was that week, etc.

People sometimes love their first tint, but they'll never see that same color again because they'll never be working with the same hair. The tint itself penetrates the hair shaft, swells it up and breaks it down chemically, so that every time they tint, they're working with different hair.

The only time you can really come close to guessing what color you're going to wind up with is when you're working with virgin hair that's never been treated. You usually see that kind of hair once—the first time. After that, you're taking your chances. The structure and condition of hair is chemically changed when it's tinted. It's changed even further if it's exposed to sun, the environment, or perms. Not only must you condition it more, you're never working with exactly the same hair so you're never quite sure how the tint will affect it.

Anyway, I tried for years to get this color that the analyst had suggested to me. Sometimes I'd come close, but it was never quite right.

Then a friend who really knew about color analysis kept urging me to let my own natural color grow out. I was this gorgeous thirty-nine-year-old bleached blonde and she wanted me to go through the excruciating process of letting my hair grow out. To make a very long story short, I did and my natural color, which I hadn't see in about twenty years, turned out to be exactly the light ash brown that the first color analyst had said would be perfect for me.

## Freedom

I cannot tell you how good it felt to have my own hair, and it wasn't just that it was the perfect color. Something happened to me inside when I took that step. Not only was I free of the trouble and expense of coloring my hair, not only did I have an absolutely perfect color, but I felt a tremendous feeling of joy and expansion. I realized that, all along, my own real hair had been not only all right, but the very best color for me. A huge weight lifted off my shoulders, and I felt like a new person— younger, lighter, freer, and much happier.

Of course, after that I got very righteous for a while and refused to color anyone's hair. I even refused for a time to cut people's hair if they'd had it tinted. I worked with a lot of people who were willing to grow out their hair in order to keep coming to me, and I was able to nurse them through the process because of my own experience. Nine times out of ten, they were thrilled with the real color of their hair—no matter how agonizing the process of growing it out had been.

I'm not on such a high horse about coloring these days, but I do ask people to choose carefully before they color their hair, and to rechoose each time they do it.

It's not that coloring or tinting is bad; it's just that, when they start, people aren't aware of the ramifications. Here's how a lifetime of hair coloring can get started just because a woman didn't take the time to think about what she was doing.

## The Habit

Sandy was a twenty-five-year-old housewife with two young kids, and not at all concerned about grey hair. One dull, rainy afternoon she just got fed up with her boring, mousey hair and her boring, mousey life. She was feeling left out, bogged down, and she needed to do something on a whim.

She went to the drugstore, looked around at the colors on the bottles, and grabbed one off the shelf. The directions just said "wash in" so it didn't sound like anything too serious and besides, she needed something to get her out of her rut. This nice reddish color seemed like just the thing. She figured that if she didn't like it, she could always go back to her old color.

As it turns out, she didn't get a "wash away" color or even a five-week rinse that would wash out more slowly. She got a real, double-bottle tint that involved peroxide, and color that penetrated the hair shaft and was never, ever going to wash out. If she ever wanted to stop being this new color, she was going to have to let her own hair grow out.

Even when she realized this, it was still okay. Not so bad, anyway. She got four or five compliments on it and, after all, it was a change. The problems started about six weeks later, when she started to see *roots*. About a half-inch of "boring, mousey" old color had grown out and presented a definite contrast with the red. Not only that, but she and her husband were going to a dinner party in three days and she had to do *something*. She figured, "Well, I can let my own color grow back later. I have to do something about the roots *now*".

After the dinner party, Sandy had a couple of options (these options get more or less complicated and expensive, depending on whether you colored light to dark, or dark to light):

1. She could tint the tinted part back to her natural color, and just wait for it all to grow out.

2. She could simply let the roots grow out and have two-toned hair for a year.

3. She could keep coloring.

Sandy kept coloring and now, twenty years later, she has a habit. She never even thinks about options anymore. She just goes in every so often and has it done. It doesn't matter if she doesn't have time or if they can't really afford it—or even if it's the right color for her. It has to be done, and she doesn't question it any more than she questions brushing her teeth.

## How It Starts, and Continues

The number one reason people color their hair is that they started without knowing what they were getting into, without considering the consequences, and then never found the right time or were willing to put up with the discomfort of growing their hair out. It became a habit, and now they do it without even thinking about it.

Another way people get into coloring is that they go to the beauty salon one morning when both they and their lives are looking awful, plop down in the chair and say, "God, I feel so yucky I just don't know what to do." The stylist brightens up and says, "Well, why don't we just spark you up a little." From that moment on, they're off and running on the color treadmill.

Sometimes people start coloring because they have a mate who's younger than they are—or is starting to *look* a lot younger than they do. Again, it's the fear of looking older, and especially the fear of looking older than our mates.

Others consider stopping, but then say, "Yeah, but I could never stop tinting (stripping, tipping, streaking) my hair because that's the only thing that gives my hair body!" I say, "Yes, but is it worth looking like you're wearing a zebra hat every day?" These techniques have to be done with a high degree of skill to be in good taste and look anywhere near natural.

There are a lot of other ways to give hair more body. You don't have to do things to your hair that aren't part of your natural harmony. People don't really notice whether your hair has body, but they do notice when the color of your hair isn't in line with the rest of you. If it isn't, the result is a mild shock that puts everything out of synch.

Tipping hair was very popular a while back. It was a little better than tinting because it only put in streaks of color, usually a very light color, and you didn't have this skull cap of black roots in a few weeks.

It was also better because, although the initial investment was substantial, you didn't have to do it as often. The trouble was that it only looked natural if you had blonde streaks in your hair to begin with. When brunettes tried tipping their hair, whether they used blonde or reddish streaks, it looked like the zebra hat again. The other problem was that people started getting stuck again in having to have it in order to give their hair body.

Coloring your hair isn't intrinsically bad. It's not just a way for the beauty industry to make money, but I hate to see people coloring their hair simply out of habit, or because they don't know what else to do, or because they've never been given permission *not* to do it, or because they simply haven't taken the time to rechoose—and rechoose correctly each time.

When women look back to see why they first started coloring their hair, the reasons are almost never valid anymore. Maybe their husband liked redheads, but now he's no longer alive—or has run off with a natural redhead.

When you try a new food, you figure out whether you like it and rechoose about whether to buy it the next time you're in the store. We often don't give ourselves that same opportunity with something as important as the color of our hair.

*When Tinting Works*

I always urge people to let their hair grow out just to see how it feels. Then if they'd rather go back to coloring it, great. They've made a conscious choice and they know what they're doing.

Tinting is also fine for people like my seventy-two-year-old friend who's so full of life, and knows herself so well, that she'd never do anything just out of habit or because she was afraid of the alternative. This woman's hair is mostly grey now, but she was a redhead when she was younger and now she tints it a reddish color. On her, it looks fine.

It looks fine because she wears it with her head held high, has herself together, and knows what it is to be alive and take a stand. When it comes to hair color, she takes a stand for "reddish." She's not using the tint as a *substitute* for anything. She tints her hair because she likes the way it looks, and if other people don't like it, that's too bad. There's no hint of insecurity about her!

*Investigate the Consequences*

If people feel they just have to color their hair, I usually recommend that they either: 1) just do the part of their hair they're concerned with (if that's possible and the area is selected carefully), or 2) use a rinse that washes out in several weeks.

In any case, the most important thing is to investigate the consequences and ramifications of anything you're considering doing. Don't just take the "bare bones" informaltion I've presented here and assume you know all about hair coloring. Ask your stylist. Know what you're putting on your hair before you do it.

And remember, don't color your hair to avoid anything. Do it because you want to, not because you need to. Be sure you know exactly what you're getting into, and choose a color that's close to your own and in harmony with the rest of you.

*Going to the Salon*

Many people in my seminars share that going to the beauty

salon is a harrowing experience. They fear it, dread it, avoid it, postpone it, and bemoan it. This section is about getting exactly what you want when you go to the salon, having a wonderful time while you're there, and creating a positive experience for both you and your stylist.

My friend Sarah, who's fifty, complained about going to a salon to get her hair styled and being treated as if she were invisible. She said they paid little attention to her, and she felt very insignificant. The stylist barely asked her what she wanted, and when she finally told him, he just started cutting as if he didn't have any idea that she was a real person, a vital individual who counted on the planet. Sarah was not only angry, but puzzled by the experience—and it wasn't the first time it had happened.

When she told me about it, I asked her what she had worn. "Oh, just an old jogging suit," she said. "No makeup. I wanted to be comfortable, and wasn't about to try and present an 'important' image. I didn't want to change clothes, and anyway, why should I dress up just to get my hair cut?"

You dress up to get your hair cut because if you don't take your appearance seriously, neither will the stylist. Sarah's casual approach was probably where the trouble started. She'd never been to that particular salon before, and they didn't know her. The statements you make about yourself by how you dress and act are very important, especially the first time you go to a salon.

## What Happens With Stylist

Like many other people in service-oriented professions, hair stylists should examine closely why they're there. If they are really there to serve people and give them what they want—and if they *realize* that's what the profession is about—then they're going to have the time of their lives. All day, they have people around them whose lives they can transform. It can be the most exhilarating, satisfying, and delightful thing in the world.

By the same token, the days can get very long and difficult for people in service-oriented professions who haven't yet discovered what a joy it is to serve people, and who are just coming to work to collect a paycheck, do a job, and see what's in it for them.

Unless they've found out what a pleasure it is to contribute to and uplift everyone they touch, there's a temptation to view clients as interruptions, annoyances and nuisances—and not to get real excited about earnest, honest people who just want to look good, unless those people are either very beautiful and fashionable, or very facinating.

THIS IS PARTICULARLY TRUE WITH OLDER PEOPLE. The older you are, the more effort you need to make to be dressed nicely, to be clear and assertive about what you want, to be secured about who you are, and to look current when you go to the salon.

That's what you're up against, and it doesn't do you any good to say, "Well, then it's all their fault."

The best solution, obviously, is to find a salon you like, where people treat you with understanding, warmth and respect, and where they listen to what you want and give it to you. If you haven't found that yet, keep looking. They're out there. There are many, many salons dedicated to serving their clients, being creative, and upholding very high ethical standards. When you find them, they're worth their weight in gold.

Look for a stylist with whom you feel comfortable. Be sure he/she listens to you. Communication is of the essence. Find someone who will spend five to fifteen minutes consulting with you about your wants and needs. Beware of someone who won't let you get a word in edgewise. It's easy to get into ego struggles with people like that, and it doesn't do either of you any good. It's your money; you deserve to be heard.

On the other hand, don't go to the salon with the idea of putting your stylist to a test. Don't lean back with your arms folded, figuring he'll do a bad job, and say to yourself, "I'll just wait and see how it turns out." Neither of you benefits from that, either. You need to participate in the process. Be honest and open with the stylist, direct about what you want, willing to take some time to talk about it, and open to new styles and ideas. Just because one stylist may have been untrustworthy or intimidating doesn't mean that they're all that way.

You may even need to talk to your stylist about what your fears are and the things that haven't worked for you in the past. You may also want to mention the things that *have* worked for you.

It usually helps to bring in a picture and show it to them. If it's realistic (the person's face, lines and hair are similar to yours), it can be a big help in communicating what you want.

Beware of the tendency to want to make a change, but not to look different from the way you looked before.

If you haven't found all this in a salon and stylist quite yet, there are some things you can do in the meantime.

## Making It Work For You

There are several things you can do to have the best experience possible at the salon.

1.  The way to be successful at the beauty salon the first time out is to look terrific when you go in. If you come in looking scruffy, as if you don't really care about your appearance anyway, why should they go out of their way to make you look terrific?

2.  Don't walk as if you're ashamed to be there, don't know what to do, and don't really think they can do much with you anyway. They'll figure they can get away with giving you nothing more than clean hair and a cut that doesn't matter to you. They may not go out of their way to be creative, because you won't know the difference—or care.

If, on the other hand, you come in looking great and feeling great about the way you look, they see you through different eyes entirely. You command respect. You *deserve* a good job. You *deserve* all of their attention and creativity for the hour you are there.

They'll look at you the same way you look at yourself, for better or worse. If they get a sense that you're a woman who knows what she's about, is there for herself and her self-expression, they'll listen to what you want and give you their all.

3.  Give of yourself. Forget about your own fear and open up to these people. Let them know who you are and what you want done with your hair. Let them see you. Hiding doesn't work. It just makes you invisible and gives them another excuse not to do their best.

## The Giveaway

You may dress nicely, walk in with a presence that indicates you are secure and assertive, and be unbelievably open, but there's one way to blow the whole thing.

A woman can do all these things, but if she walks in with a bubble hairdo that's ratted and teased a foot away from her head, they are not going to get the impression that this is a person who stays very current. The same is true for someone who's wearing a hippie skirt and Birkenstock sandals. People in the salon will figure that, somewhere along the way, these women got stuck.

Probably the strongest negative statement you can make when you walk into a salon is, "I'm not current and I don't care to be." You'd never say those words, but you don't have to. If you have gotten stuck somewhere, or for some reason just stopped being current, it's the first thing they'll pick up about you.

*Being In Charge*

If you place the responsibility for whether or not you leave the salon with what you wanted on yourself, rather than on the people in the salon, you'll get what you want.

Don't expect much if you walk in thinking, "Well, I've done my job. I've shown up. Now it's up to them because they're the experts and I don't know anything." Be responsible for taking some time before you go in, getting centered, and knowing exactly what you want. Then take it upon yourself to tell them what that is. You may want to bring in a picture for them to use as a guideline. They can't read minds, and it's not fair to expect them to come up with exactly what you want without being told. It's a guessing game you can't win.

Stylists are trained in all the technical aspects of working with hair, and in the artistic design of cutting. Make the best use of their training and talent by giving them every advantage you can.

When you go into the salon, you're spending your time and money. You want to take away what you came for. It's almost like a business deal or contract. Be sure you make the most of it, and give the stylist every advantage you can so he or she can do a good job for you.

Some people go around testing salons. They walk in and want to be "done." Then they're disappointed when they don't get what they want. These are the people who say, "I just can't find people who can do my hair right. No one cares or listens."

The interesting thing is this: The one consistent element in this scenario of bad experiences at salons is the individual. You, as the client, have to be the one who makes sure they listen, and who makes sure you communicate.

If you went to the butcher and asked for a pound of hamburger, and he started to give you three lamb chops, would you just meekly put them in your sack, pay for them and walk away? Don't do that at salons, either. You're entering into a business agreement with these people. Be sure both of you keep your end of the bargain.

Look your best. Present yourself nicely. Get into communication with them. Tell them what you want. If they suggest something you don't like, tell them so. Convince them it's worth their while to work on you and be creative about your hairstyle. Be the one in charge of the results. Manage them as you might a contractor coming to put a porch on your house. Don't just close your eyes and hope for the best. Make sure you get a clear picture or idea of what you've both talked about and agreed upon. Then you both win.

### Staying Open: Change, Variety and Staying Current

I'm convinced that one of the most important things you can do to avoid falling into the Polluted Pond is to stay open, to accept a variety of looks for yourself, and to stay current with fashion. It's also one of the best ways to get other people to respect you and listen to you.

By being current, I don't mean being faddish or bizarre, or giving yourself over to punk. I just mean looking like you belong in the world today, and not ten, twenty, thirty or forty years ago.

When you get stuck in particular ways of looking, acting and thinking, you automatically date yourself. Not only does that prevent you from growing and enjoying what is here today, but it tells other people that talking to you and being with you can only be a lesson in history.

Being outdated also tends to make us insecure and intimidated, especially in places like popular, top-ranking salons. A particular look may have been comfortable back then when it was in style, but we're almost never really comfortable looking like we belong somewhere in the past.

I know it can be tricky. Friends hardly ever mention this sort of thing, because they're used to seeing us a certain way. We're sometimes afraid to change because we don't really know what to do and are afraid of looking ridiculous. We think we have to go punk, or jump on the lastest fad, in order to be current and allow for some variety.

58

This is definitely not the case. You can dress stylishly and in good taste, and also be very current. Take some time to find out how to do it if you don't have a sense yourself. You may have to invest a little time, but you don't have to invest much money. Having your colors done, which we'll discuss in a later chapter, is the perfect place to start. It's the best investment you can make in your appearance.

I've seen people leaf through magazines and say, "YUCK," to everything they see that isn't exactly like what they have on. This is a dangerous game. Not only does it close off options, but if nothing is right except your current idea of what's right, then you'll never be in fashion. You don't have to like everything you see, but look at it and appreciate it for what it is. You may have it on next year, so don't be too quick to criticize.

To stay current and allow for a variety of looks, you have to take risks. Maybe that's what's so attractive about people who are willing to do it. I don't know. I do know that whether a person looks current or not is just about the number one clue to whether they're thinking and acting in the present, rather than in the past.

*SECRET #5*: BE OPEN TO A VARIETY OF STYLES AND IDEAS, AND BE WILLING TO STAY CURRENT.

Have fun trying new things. All life changes and grows. We never stay the same. Wearing different clothing, doing different things, being with different people are just indications that we're moving and growing. It's not something we can do once, and be through with it. This openness is something that makes us feel creative and alive at any age.

# 7.
# GREY HAIR

*Why People Tint Grey Hair*
In the last chapter, we talked about why people color their hair. Now we'll look specifically at why people color *grey* hair. These are some of the reasons:

1. *Grey is old, and nobody wants that*! The most common reason is that, after decades of advertising and conditioning, most of us

have bought the idea that grey hair is the symbol of this awful thing called aging. There's a stigma attached to grey hair in some people's minds, and that stigma creates a fear that, now that they have grey hair, all the other things people believe about older people are also true of them.

"Oh my God, a grey hair!" they shriek, and run to the drugstore for a bottle of hair color or Geritol, depending on whether they're inclinded to resist aging or succumb to it.

2. *Habit*. Another reason people tint their grey hair is that they've *always* tinted their hair. We talked about these people in the last chapter. They aren't even sure they have grey hair, but keep tinting just in case it's grey. It doesn't matter *what* color their hair is; they're going to keep tinting no matter what.

Even the cost doesn't stop them. These people will find a way, even if they have to take the money out of the food budget. Everything else in their lives may be falling apart, especially as they get older, but at least they have this one thing, their hair, handled—and it's going to stay handled at any cost. These people will keep coloring their hair into their nineties and put in their wills, "Be sure to do my roots before you put me in the coffin."

Often these people started with a color that was in fashion when they began coloring their hair, but has long since ceased to be "in." This produces the opposite of what they want; it actually makes them look older.

3. *Husbands*. A lot of women tint their hair because they think they'd be less attractive to their husbands with grey hair. When I suggest to them that they let it grow out, they purse their lips and say, "Well, I don't know what Jimmy would think about *that!*" A lot of women are afraid they won't be sexually attractive, and that their husbands will start thinking of them as old.

The surprising truth is that most husbands really don't care. These wives are using their husbands as an excuse not to let their grey grow in. The men would just as soon their wives went grey. This was a shock to me at first, but I've talked to many, many men about it and they really don't have much preference in this area. In fact, they haven't given it much thought or attention. They didn't marry these women expecting that they'd look twenty years old for the next fifty or sixty years, and really don't define beauty, or even youth, in terms of hair color nearly as much as women do.

When women let their grey hair grow in, they often get the added benefit of finding that their husbands still love them—much more than they thought—and that it has nothing to do with the color of their hair.

4. *Hairstylists.* Sometimes hair stylists talk people into tinting their grey hair. It's not always that they just want to make more money; they may like experimenting with colors, they may honestly think it would make the woman look better, or they may have just bought the notion that grey is old and old is bad.

## My Grey Hair

I spoke in the last chapter about my own experience with letting my hair grow out. Sometimes it was excruciating. I had to give up this bleached blonde image I had been projecting, and deal with friends who said, "Aren't you afraid of looking OLD?" But the rewards were more than I had ever hoped for. It was okay to be me!

Not only did my own color work in perfect harmony with the rest of me—my eyes, skin and general presence—but I gained a tremendous sense of freedom. I started to get a very comfortable feeling inside. It was almost as if I were whispering to myself, "You mean, it's really okay to walk around just the way I am? I don't have to cover up, or change, or hide, or add or subtract anything?" And the answer came back, "YES!" It was incredibly satisfying to know that I could get along in the world without that kind of camouflage.

Other people noticed, too. Sometimes they didn't even notice that I'd let my hair grow out. They just squinted their eyes and said things like, "Wow, what are you doing? You look so young and fabulous, so together!" Part of this was that people's eyes always seek harmony, and my natural color hair was more naturally harmonious than the tint. I think a larger part came from the way I felt about myself.

I see this same thing in most older women who let their grey grow out. They lighten up and take on a new vitality. It almost looks as if lines and wrinkles disappear, though of course they don't. They look alive, free and vibrant because, somewhere inside, they know they don't have to hide anymore.

## A Grey Designed Just For You

Another reason these women look better is that their own

natural, individual coloring is back in place. People think that grey hair is grey hair, that there's only one color of grey and you're stuck with it forever whether it goes with the rest of you or not. Not true! Grey is a myriad (and a miracle) of shadows.

Each of us has her own special color of grey hair, and that unique color is in absolute harmony with the rest of our coloring. This is why it's so easy to throw the whole picture out of whack by tinting our hair, and why the blue rinses people used to put on grey never really worked.

People used those blue rinses because they were afraid their grey was "yellowish." Sometimes grey hair turns a little yellowish if it's exposed to cigarette smoke or other pollutants, but unless that's the case, any tinge of "yellow" you find in your hair probably belongs there.

Your own grey was designed specifically for you. The key is to get in touch with your own resonance or harmony, and choose clothing and makeup that accents and enhances the grey, as well as your eye color and skin tones.

### Questions To Ask Yourself

How do you decide whether or not to keep coloring your grey hair? If you do it, you should be going *toward* something rather than *away from* something. If you're coloring your hair because you're afraid of something, don't do it. Here are some questions you might want to ask yourself:

1. Did someone like my hairstylist originally talk to me into coloring my hair? Is that selection still valid today?
2. Do a few grey hairs scare me?
3. Do I avoid grey in order not to look old?
4. Does my present color truly satisfy me, or am I just doing it out of habit?
5. If I could color or not color, without considering anyone except myself, what would I do?
6. Does this color serve my total individual look?
7. Does it say what I want to be saying about myself?
8. Is it really attractive?
9. Is it harmonious with the color of my skin and eyes?
10. When was the last time I saw my natural color?

### Making the Break

Suppose you've decided you've had it with coloring your grey hair and are going to let it all grow out. I know it's not easy. I know you can't just decide one afternoon never to dye your hair again, and never have any problems after that. If you decide to make the break, you'll have all sorts of challenges.

First, you're going to look different from the way you looked before. You will probably look better, but any change is difficult at first. You'll have to get used to the new you, and give yourself permission to feel a little awkward about it from time to time.

Second, your friends may give you some trouble, particularly if they're still tinting their own grey hair. It may be threatening to them for you to do something different. It may remind them of all the time and money they spend on their own hair, and the lack of freedom that they feel. It may be that they envy your courage, or are afraid you'll look better than they do.

They may say, "Aren't you afraid of looking older?" To which you can reply, "Maybe I will, but I'll be able to handle that if it comes up. For now, I'm just going to stick with what I've decided to do."

When they said that to me, I thought to myself, "Well, maybe I'm going to look *ancient*, but I'm going to be the most sexy, attractive, feminine, gorgeous, vibrant ancient old lady ever." I decided that just because I had grey hair didn't mean I couldn't look good. It didn't mean I couldn't have fun. Where did I ever get the idea that it did? I created a new mission for myself—being grey and feeling attractive.

Your friends may say, "You know, I really don't think you should do this. I think you're going to be sorry." That's when you really have to be on your toes. Remember, you're doing this for *you*, and not to please anybody else. The odds are that you won't please people, but remember that anything they say is probably a reflection of their own insecurities, and not something you have to take as gospel truth.

Just let the negative comments bounce off you, and stay in touch with why you're doing this. I find it's best not to get defensive with people, but to recognize what they say is true for them and allow them to have their opinions.

One way to handle just about anything is to respond, "You know, you may be right. I really don't know if I'm going to like it, but I haven't seen my own color in twenty years and I've got to do this." That gives them a chance to retreat without being wrong. They can get off your back without losing the battle.

If even that doesn't work, you can always say, "I'd rather not talk about this. I'm a little nervous about it myself, and this kind of conversation just makes it harder."

You don't have to make other people wrong, but you should let them know that you're taking a stand. You might even want to start a buddy system. I have many clients for whom I'm on 24-hour call. They can call me any time they're tempted to "hit the bottle"—the tint bottle, that is.

*Why Grey is Beautiful*

A good ninety-five percent of all the people I've talked into letting their grey hair grow out are delighted with the results, and thank me over and over again. They say it was worth every second of discomfort, because they have a part of themselves back. Not only that, but they see they truly are more attractive with grey hair than with whatever color they were using.

Some of the advantages of letting grey hair grow out are obvious:

1. You put yourself back into your natural color harmonies.
2. You let yourself be how you really are.
3. You save time and money, and avoid being a slave to the tint bottle.
4. The condition of your hair improves.

An advantage that's perhaps less obvious is that something wonderful happens inside when you take a stand for yourself and go back to your own natural hair color. People say, "Wow, what's come over you?" They can't quite put their finger on what it is, but they know there's been a big change for the better.

There's something tremendously empowering about being all of yourself, and it doesn't confine itself to the color of your hair. That's usually just the first step. I've seen women start whole new lives and careers out of the courage they found in dealing with the color of their hair.

It's also very empowering to make a choice and stick to it, even in the face of opposition. When that choice involves giving yourself permission to be exactly the way you are, both physically and emotionally, it's even more satisfying.

All I want is for people to give grey hair a chance, especially if they're over fifty. I want for them to be willing to make an honest choice about it. I can practically guarantee that they'll be delighted with the results, and I know they'll free up more than time and money. They'll rediscover and learn to appreciate a precious part of themselves.

*SECRET #6:* TAKE A STAND FOR YOURSELF.

Trust yourself and your instincts. Tell the truth about yourself, whether it's the things you like to do or the color of your hair. Be true to yourself, and let the chips fall where they may.

# 8.
# EXPRESSING YOUR PERSONAL ESSENCE

*What Is Your Personal Essence?*
The words have been around for years. We say, "Oh yeah, personal essence, personal style..." Then our minds drift toward people who are rich, or models, or in the public eye, or in some other way deserving of having some spiffy "personal essence" created just for them by someone in Hollywood.

And even if we thought we should or could have one, how would we go about getting a personal style?

First, let's look at what it means to express your personal essence. To me, it means two things. One is more artistic and technical; the other has to do with inner substance and how we think about ourselves.

*Color, Line and Texture*
Perhaps the most important element of personal style, when we're talking about artistic and technical aspects, is color. "Having your colors done" is becoming a common activity. The business of "doing people's colors" was even written up in *The Wall Street Journal.* What happens, more or less, is that the color analyst sits with you in natural light, with no makeup, and selects anywhere from about thirty to hundreds of colors that are harmonious with your own natural coloring.

The analyst rarely picks only reds for you and says you should never wear blue. Usually he or she chooses a special range of tints and hues within each basic color, and suggests how they might be put together.

People generally fall into basic groups of colors. Some people call these "harmonies" (soft, rich, striking, or animated), some call them seasons (summer, fall, winter, or spring), and some divide them in other ways. Most people have aspects of at least two of these groups. You might be sixty-five percent summer, for instance, and thirty-five percent spring. Knowing about these harmonies or groupings allows you to choose clothing that creates a total look and appears to have been designed with just you in mind.

Color analysts are now available all over the country. I have a favorite group in Oakland, California whom I recommend, and can send you information about them if you contact me through Kay's Collective, 458 Santa Clara Avenue, Oakland, California 94610.

The physical and artistic side of personal essence also involves design lines. Your design lines indicate whether you should wear round or pointed collars, long or short collars; textures that are satiny or natural; what type of jewelry (brass, gold, silver, etc.) you should choose so that everything about your appearance is harmonious. The idea is for nothing to jar or distract from what people are really interested in, which is you. You wear your clothes; they don't wear you.

Design lines even apply to hair. Do you look best in round ringlets, geometric lines, or a soft, languid wave pattern? Should your look have a smooth texture, or a spikey effect? If you choose the wrong one, an awkward sense emerges from your total look. People may not know exactly what's wrong, but something is definitely out of alignment.

When you use your own colors, lines and textures, everything about your appearance is pleasant and satisfying. The eye always seeks harmony, unity, and things that go together. Anything else is almost a mild shock to the system. When I look at someone who has learned these elements of personal style, I get a sense of well-being and peace inside. I feel good without knowing exactly why.

There are lots of people out there doing colors, however, whose main qualification is that they're interested in it. They have very little training, less skill with people, and simply no idea how to put everything together so that you come away with a total look that's uniquely designed for you. You're more apt to come away with a bunch of pretty color swatches, many of which happen to look nice on you, and no way to use them in your life.

When you decide to work with someone on color, lines and textures, check out their credentials. Find out where they went to school and what they studied, and what their experience has been. Getting the *wrong* colors is worse than getting no colors at all. Just as your own colors create a sense of harmony and resonance, surrounding yourself with the wrong colors creates a sense of discord, uneasiness and struggle.

One thing to watch for is whether the person who does your colors gives you power or takes it away from you. People who pretend that they're the experts and you're dumb because you don't understand all this may not have your best interests at heart. They may create more doubts than they take away.

The person you work with should empower you. You should walk away with a real sense of what is right for you and what is not, and be able to use it every day of your life. You should have such a strong sense of your own colors and harmonies that you can use them creatively forever. In the end, how you feel about the results is the only valid criterion.

*Saving Money*

Now I know what you're thinking: "Oh NO, I can't afford to throw out everything in my closet and start from scratch. I can't even afford a new skirt!" All I can say is that I've spent less money, and spent it more wisely, since I learned these tools than I did when I was using the "shotgun method" for selecting clothes and accessories.

When you know what you're doing, you choose things that you'll be able to wear for a long, long time. Those colors are always going to be your colors. You're making better investments, and they don't have to be expensive. I still have a belt and wear it regularly; I bought it for five dollars, fifteen years ago.

You shop smarter when you know your colors, lines and textures. You don't make the kinds of mistakes I used to make—like buying a $200 suit I only wore once because it was just the wrong color for me. When you use this approach, you almost never throw things out or give them away until they're absolutely threadbare.

Not only do you save money, you save time. In a sense, you become your own designer. You know immediately what will be wonderful on you, and what won't. Shopping and decision making become easy, pleasant and fun. You make your choices with great certainty, and pick items you love when you get home.

I wouldn't know where to begin in a store if I didn't have these tools. No wonder people hate to shop! If you don't know your colors, lines and textures, you continually wonder if you're trying on the right things, and how they're going to fit with the rest of your wardrobe. You think about whether a particular item will look good on you, and whether it's going to stay in fashion. This is a situation guaranteed to create frustration, fatigue and resentment.

It's not much help to look in *more* stores, *more* magazines, *more* ads, either. You can get lots of suggestions, but you still have no way of knowing what's right for you.

I'm sure we could all figure out our own personal styles for ourselves, without the aid of color consultants—if we just had about twenty years to sit alone in a cave and meditate about nothing but our personal essence. The reason working with color analysts has been such a blessing to me is that I'm not interested in spending ten years learning all there is to know about colors and skin tones and design lines and textures. I'd rather just go to the experts and get the best advice I can—quickly. It's saved me more time, effort and money than I can say.

### The Universal System

The beauty of this system is that it doesn't matter if you're a man or a woman, adult or child, fat or thin, light or dark. Everybody has their own colors, their own best lines, textures that are great on them, and their own unique way of putting together a visual personal essence. At this point, I can't imagine anyone trying to dress nicely on a limited budget without these tools.

I learned them twenty-five years ago, use them every day of my life, and they've grown more precious as I've gotten older. They've made my own aging process so much more painless than it might have been, and allowed me to keep choosing clothes with a great sense of certainty, direction and grace.

The best part is, not only does it look nice from the outside, to people who are looking at me, but I feel better. That sense of harmony and resonance is with me all the time, all over me, and I get to enjoy it more than anyone.

*Your Own Unique Essence*

Another aspect of expressing your personal essence has more to do with how you approach life and how you approach yourself.

We all know people who have a certain style about them. It may not even be particularly glamorous or flamboyant. They just have a sense of themselves and how they want to approach their lives and the people with whom they relate. Whatever they do or say has a certain unique flavor about it.

You find yourself thinking of them. You might walk through a store and think, "Isn't that just the type of blouse Fran would wear!" They do things in a certain way. They aren't always predictable, but after you've been around them a while you have a very clear sense of how they think about things, how they interact with strangers and friends, the kinds of things they like and don't like, and what their response is likely to be in any given situation.

You have a sense of what they think about themselves and how they relate to themselves, whether they're forgiving about not doing the breakfast dishes or whether without getting their "to do lists" done, whether they'll invite ten people to dinner on the spur of the moment, or need a few weeks to plan a candlelight event.

You know if they're likely to show up to your house for coffee in a funny hat, or speak to the checkout girl about her sick cat. You know if they'll sweep into a cocktail party dressed to the nines, or make an excuse and go watch the sunset instead.

Whatever their personal essence is, you have a sense that *they* are the ones who are creating their lives, rather than just letting themselves be pushed around by circumstances or "waiting to see what happens." You have a sense of their dominion over their lives. They don't necessarily control every detail, but they approach life from the point of view that they are in charge and they can paint whatever they want on this canvas. They're not just surviving, they're creating. They're expressing themselves in everything they say, do and wear.

The question that always comes up about people who have a strong personal essence is "HOW DO THEY GET THAT WAY?"

*Creating Your Personal Essence*

People who are good at expressing their personal essence have usually given it some thought. They haven't just sat back and hope it started oozing out of them. They've *created* it. Personal essence isn't something that's handed out at birth to some, and not to others. We all have it. Some people just develop and express it more fully than others.

It's not so much a matter of sitting down and making lists of things you're going to do and not do, say and not say, wear and not wear. It's more a question of giving yourself permission to let that next layer of you emerge and express itself in the world—and that may require some special time to sit down and just think about it. You might want to ponder such questions as:

• If I were to get a picture in my mind's eye of just how I'd like to be in the world, how I'd like to see myself, what would it look like?

• What are the ruts I'm in, and what do I want to do about them?

• What are the things I'd like to give myself permission to be, do and say that I'm currently not giving myself permission to be, do and say?

• When I think of myself as a person with my own unique style of living, what does that style look like?

These questions are just to get the ball rolling. More will occur to you as you start letting your own personal essence emerge. It's there already. All you have to do is let it out, and allow yourself to express it, even when other people are watching.

### Five-Second Meditation

There are many ways to begin creating your own personal essence. One exercise you can do at home on your own is Your Ideal Self. Another is the Five-Second Meditation, in which you just close your eyes for five seconds sometime during the day and envision yourself just the way you want to be—the way you want to look, act, feel, speak, and be with others and yourself. You can do it for longer than five seconds if you wish. The longer you do it, the better results you'll get.

Some people are afraid to try this because all the things they want to be, do, say and wear are "too young." Maybe that's a clue. Maybe you're acting older than you need to act. You might want to give yourself permission to be "too young," if that's what you'd really like to do. It's always scary to look at parts of ourselves with which we're not familiar. It may be the scariest

70

thing in the world. The rewards are rich, though. We get to be more of ourselves—and the more of ourselves we are, the more people are drawn to us.

## Side Benefits

I've found that creating an effective way of expressing personal essence is also good business. I want people to trust me in my work. If I showed up wearing curlers in my hair and a felt skirt with poodles on it, I wouldn't inspire a lot of trust. In my business, I need to be current and fashionable, but I also want people to know that I'm down-to-earth, professional and care about them. The way I dress, wear makeup, and present myself helps me make those statements.

My friend Jean wanted a job that happened to require an extremely efficient and capable person. Jean is efficient and capable, but she also took some care to dress and present herself that way, and told me she actually became *more* efficient and capable as a result.

Look at it this way. We're making statements to the world all the time—whether we know it or not, and whether we like it or not. People make decisions about us all the time, and those decisions are based largely on what we're telling them about ourselves. Expressing our own personal essence is just a way of *choosing* which statement we want to make, and aligning them with who we really are.

## Remember Your Ideal Self

It's really just a question of keeping current with your Ideal Self, of asking yourself the questions over and over until the answers become a part of you, and you become the answers.

- How do you want to relate to people?
- How do you want to feel about yourself?
- What kinds of statements do you want to make?
- What activities do you want to pursue?
- What are your goals?
- How do you want to be, alone, and as a person in the world?

Some people do this exercise every year. Others do it every month. Some people do it every day. When your Ideal Self is in your conscious awareness, you grow and bend toward it naturally, like a plant toward sunlight. Just placing that picture in your mind seems to begin the process of making it a reality.

This exercise is just as valid at the age of eighty-five as it is at fifteen—perhaps more so. Every moment of your life is a possibility, an opportunity to be more of yourself and enjoy life more fully. Why not go for it?

## It's Not Vanity; It's Good Sense

We all draw conclusions about people, consciously or unconsciously, based on what they wear and how they present themselves. Other people do the same with us. The way we put ourselves together—physically, emotionally, in every way—says a lot about what we think of ourselves. People are likely to follow our cue. If they sense that we think highly of ourselves, then so will they.

Remember, we're always projecting some sort of image. Why not choose what that image will be? Why not let it reflect who we really are, make the statements we want to make, and enjoy it in the process?

People resist creating and expressing their own personal essence for several reasons. One is that they don't believe that they deserve to have one. (They forget they have one anyway; it's just not conscious or chosen.) They think personal essence is something for the people *out there*, the people with money, position, fabulous looks, self-esteem, access to the fashion centers, and knowledge about where even to start. Believe me, if you had to have all those things—or any of them—in order to have a personal style, there wouldn't be much of it around.

Others don't begin because they don't know where to start. There are many places you can start. You can set aside an hour to do nothing but sit quietly and think about it. You can look through magazines or stores. You can see a competent color analyst. Most importantly, you can just start giving yourself permission to let that style emerge.

Some people say, "Oh, I just don't know anything about that. I don't know what to do." We were taught when we were young, and have continued to be told all our lives, that we don't know what we're doing. Most of us have bought it, but the truth is that we *can* know. We can release that belief about "not knowing" just by adopting the point of view that we do know, and giving ourselves permission to operate in the world as if we did.

Other people are afraid that developing a personal essence is manipulative, that its purpose is to control people, to make them think and do what you want. This will only happen if that's where you're coming from. If that's not your purpose, then it won't happen.

If you let your own natural style emerge, then you're not misrepresenting yourself at all. You're just allowing the natural expression of something that is the essentially you. We're meant to enjoy life and to have fun, to be all that we can be. Self expression and choice are part of life, part of that unfolding.

Perhaps the main reason that people are reluctant to develop a personal essence is that they don't think they have a right to do it, that it would be vain and conceited for them to devote that much attention to themselves. We're taught when we're very young that we shouldn't compliment ourselves or be selfish and self-absorbed.

The result is usually that people go 180 degrees in the opposite direction. They spend a lifetime beating themselves up, refusing to look at themselves with any care or concern, or to pay attention to their wants and needs. This is an extraordinarily diminishing process. The don't have the sense of themselves and the appreciation of themselves that we are all meant to have as children of nature. The result is a lessening of life, rather than an enhancement of it. It also makes it difficult for them to love and give to others. It's very hard to give to others what you don't have for yourself.

*Trust Yourself*

Sometimes it's simply frightening to go out and do something different, to have a style that's just our own. We're often afraid that people won't like us, and yet we ourselves are usually drawn to people who have their own unique style, who have a strong sense of themselves. They don't have to be loud or flashy. There are some very quiet people who have an incredibly strong sense of themselves. When I'm around people like that, I feel good. I feel good about them, and I feel good about myself.

People who step out and do something different, who aren't afraid to be all of themselves, are exciting. When I first started letting myself be, and allowing my own personal style to emerge, I was terrified. I thought I'd lose all my friends. Amazingly enough, just the opposite happened. I found that people were really much more eager to spend time with me. I was flabbergasted, until I looked back and saw the kind of people that I enjoyed. They were also people who had taken a stand for themselves.

Give yourself a gift. Take some special time for yourself to begin developing and expressing your personal essence. Once you start, you may not be able to stop! Begin by answering these questions.

- Where are you now?
- Where do you want to be?
- What statements do you want to make to the world?
- What makes you feel good?
- If you feel good, you'll look good. What's been stopping you from having all these things?
- What are you going to do about it?

You'll be ahead of the game if you even just sit down for a few hours to think about these things, and it may just change your life.

The more you discover about your personal essence, the easier it is to communicate it. When you step out and take a stand for yourself, you allow other people to do the same thing. If you can give yourself permission, you can give them permission, too. You can have your way, and they can have theirs. No one is right; everyone just has their own way. The more you allow me to say what my way is, the better I can listen to you.

That's a very nice way to live, and it all comes from each of us being more of ourselves.

## SECRET #7: CREATE YOUR POSSIBILITIES; DON'T LIMIT THEM.

Life is nothing but possibilities. We can deny them, restrict ourselves, and try to live within some made up, out of date idea about how we should be. The other way is to live creatively, looking at what we want and enjoy, how we can contribute to ourselves, one another and the world. Being "unselfish" can be a great cloak for martyrdom. No one was ever hurt because someone became more of themselves or got better. To create and explore possibilities enhances life; to limit them denies life.

74

# 9.
# WHAT YOU CAN DO

*Plenty!*

I hate to see people shake their heads slowly from side to side, roll their eyes sadly, and say, "Well, I'm just getting older, and there's nothing I can do about it." REMEMBER, YOU'RE NEVER TOO OLD TO FEEL YOUNG.

There's nothing we can do about our chronological age, and there's no reason we should want to or have to do anything about it. We can, however, do something about *how* we grow older. This can be the most wonderful time of our lives, if we let it be. It's no accident that these are called the "harvest years." We earned them. We paid our dues; now let's enjoy them!

The main thing we can do, of course, is to keep out of the Polluted Pond. The only things in there are excuses—excuses for not being physically and mentally active, excuses for all our troubles, excuses for giving up on life.

No one is pushing us into the pond, and we don't have to fall unless we want to. There's so much else to do! There is so much life out there, just for the asking. There's so much to be, to talk about, to contribute to people. It's just ridiculous to buy the myth that life is over, or that life is less, when we are older.

Age is wisdom and experience. We can't buy these things. They're what we've earned, what we are. Let's put them to work for us. Getting older is a challenge and an opportunity. If we can begin to see it as such, this can be the most exciting time of our lives.

*Action Steps*

Each time I hear that whine, "But I can't do anything about it," I want to hand people a list. On that list would be all the things they could do to start dragging themselves out of the pond, if they wanted to.

Some of the things I'd put on that list are definite, physical things you can go out and *do*. Others are more internal ways of "being," of thinking about yourself and the world. They're all things I've tried and that have worked for me.

It's just a beginning. I'm sure other ideas will occur to you as you read. If they do, I encourage you to write them down and do them!

1. *Stand up straight.* You used to hear that when you were a kid, right? And now you're hearing it again. Yuk! You've probably said it to your children, so most likely you know the reasons. First of all, it looks better—and there's no sense in not doing things that make us look better. Second, it makes us feel better. Standing up straight frees the energy in our spine and body to move without getting stuck, or making us look like we're holding onto something inside.

I know so many people, both men and women, who look much older than they are because of their posture. If they stood up straight, they would look ten years younger.

I sometimes find myself hunching over, especially when I'm worried about something or when I'm driving. As soon as I notice it, I uncurl myself and sit or stand up straight. I imagine a string running through me like a marionette, right from my tailbone through the top of my head, and I just pull up on the string.

There's a tremendous physical release when all the muscles and bones line up straight, on top of each other the way they're supposed to be. It feels as if they all heave a sigh of relief.

Many studies suggest that imitating some particular mood with our bodies can actually make us feel that way. If you feel down in the dumps, for instance, take a walk with great, long strides, swinging your arms and smiling as if you didn't have a care in the world. Before long, you'll actually start feeling that way.

Standing and sitting up straight create the feeling—within yourself and for the outside world—that you are ready to face life with courage and joy. Nothing has beaten you down; you're ready for anything and moving forward.

2. *Keep busy.* We've all heard the stories of people who were in perfect physical and mental health until they retired. After they'd been home a few months, they seemed like different people. They became listless, uninterested, and started having health problems.

That doesn't mean people shouldn't retire, but human beings weren't intended just to sit around and vegetate. It's not our nature to be static. We want to move and grow. In fact, the wonderful thing about retirement is that it gives us a chance to move and grow in new directions.

Keeping busy sustains our interest in life, in other people, and in ourselves. Not only can we make tremendous contributions as a result of our experience, but giving to others lets us learn new things about the world and about ourselves everyday. I think every person on earth wants to contribute to others. We have rich, beautiful things to contribute, and many of us have more time now to do it.

Volunteer at the hospital, the library, the school. Take some classes. Get current on your reading. Start an exercise program. Meet new people. Go to church. Work part-time, or full-time. Catch up on old friendships. Be careful about how much TV you watch. Look in the newspaper for what's going on around town, and get involved. Take a walk and be sure you speak to at least three people. These are all ways to keep busy and involved.

Staying busy keeps your energy level high, and that's a key to feeling good and staying healthy. It's also a way of expressing yourself, of releasing your energy into the world so it doesn't get all pent up inside and make you nervous or vulnerable to disease. You feel as if you're participating in the world and contributing to it—and you are. In my opinion, there's nothing more important for maintaining your health and well-being than that.

3.  *Watch your nutrition*. No matter how good we feel mentally, emotionally and spiritually, we need to support our physical bodies in being as happy and healthy as they can be.

I'm not a nutrition expert, and I don't pretend to be able to give you a specific diet that will work for you and keep you feeling great. I do know that nutrition is vital to our well-beng, however, and think it's important for all of us to investigate what will work for us.

You are what you eat, they say. I believe it because I've lived on junk food and I've lived on food that's considered to be nut-ritious, and I can tell the difference.

The same things don't work for everybody, so you may have to do some research and exploration. One thing I do know, however, is that moisture leaves our bodies as we get older, so we have to be more careful to replace it regularly with fluids. The other thing I know is that the foods you crave are the foods to which you're addicted. It might be potato chips, wine, cheese, candy bars, cigarettes or whatever. If you find yourself having to have some particular food all the time, try going without it for a while and see what happens.

Sometimes we don't even realize we're eating a lot of food that isn't particularly good for us. When I ask people about their diet, usually in response to some problem with their hair, they generally say, "Oh, I eat real well." Then I have them actually make a list of everything they put in their mouths over a period of two weeks, and they are appalled. They had no idea they were eating that much junk food and that many empty calories. It's a good exercise if you're not really sure what you're eating.

There is a lot of information available about nutrition, and it's hard to sort it all out, but you don't need a Ph.D. to figure out some basic principles and work out a program for yourself. Experiment, and see which foods make you feel best. You don't need to completely change your diet, but if you notice that there are four giant bags of potato chips on your list each week, you might want to consider cutting down.

Remember, the whole point is to feel better, so do whatever accomplishes that result.

4. *Take risks.* I don't mean to roll the dice, or cast the *I Ching* and invest all your savings in whatever stock comes up. Taking risks, to me, means extending myself. It means speaking to someone in the market whom I don't know, smiling at someone on the street, inviting several new friends over for dinner.

It also means being more of me, whether that's letting my grey hair grow in, starting a new business, getting involved in a relationship, or changing the way I look.

Taking risks makes us grow. It's as simple as that. We stretch ourselves. We force ourselves to be more than we were before. We get bigger, more open, more trusting of ourselves. Even if some of the risks don't turn out too well, it feels good to extend ourselves.

5. *Don't be an ostrich.* Sometimes we sense that we are aging, but we refuse to really look at the issue and see what we're going to do about it. We feel ourselves on the edge of the Polluted Pond, but are afraid to take any steps to avoid falling in. It's almost as if we didn't think there was anything we could do about it.

I call this the Ostrich Response. We stick our heads in the sand and don't deal with what becomes, increasingly, the main issue in our lives. It's not that we don't worry about growing older. We do. It's just that we don't do anything about the worry. Any doctor or psychiatrist will tell you that makes for stress and tension, which in turn make the things we were worried about in the first place seem even worse.

Often people don't think they're worth the effort. "Well," they think, "I could do this or that to feel better, but who do I think I am? Why should I bother? Who's going to know or care if I get old?" The answer is: YOU ARE!

Feeling wonderful and more alive is not something for *those people over there*—the ones who are in *People Magazine*, who know about fashion, who are smarter or more prominent, richer, or who in some way have more status than we do. It's for each person on the face of this earth, every day of their lives.

Other people get a glimmer that it would be all right to feel better and more alive, to go ahead and do something about the quality of their lives, but they don't know what to do. The fear of the unknown gets to them, and they close down entirely. They say, "Ah, that was a crumby idea anyway. Who did I think I was kidding?" And they then reject anything that comes along that might make them feel more alive.

We all have a right to a full life, to a life that's creative and joyful. More than that, we have an obligation to experience as much life as we can. That's what living is about. Those rights and obligations don't go away. *You can't retire from life as long as you're alive.*

6.    *Be of service to others.* Several years ago, I had a piece of magic fall into my lap that completely changed my life. For most of my life and career, I'd been trying to "make it." To me, that meant waiting lists of four or five months, everybody delighted with what I did with their hair and telling all their friends, and generally having a lot of agreement that I was terrific and everyone should have their hair done by me.

I wanted to make it not just because of my ego, buy because I had a family to support and a lot of other expenses. My business ultimately became very successful, but I still felt this sense of struggle. For one reason or another, my attention was always on ME.

Eventually, it began to dawn on me that the way I'd set it up to have my attention on myself all the time simply didn't work. I was successful, but I wasn't happy, and somehow I didn't really have what I wanted.

I began to entertain the possibility that my life was about something more that just my own petty concerns, that it was about making a contribution to other people. As soon as I did that, something broke open. I took it a step further and realized that, not only might my life be about getting happy through serving other people, but if that were the case, I had chosen the most perfect profession in the world. Every hour of the day, I either had employees to work with or new people in my chair and could start all over again.

All of a sudden, everything got easy. I forgot about proving myself to everybody, and just concentrated on my employees and the people sitting in my chair. I got all the attention off myself simply by being interested in them and their well-being, and by being available to help them. I stopped getting fatigued, and felt terrific at the end of each day. The funny thing was that my business got even better.

People are often afraid to take their attention off themselves and put it on other people, to really be there for other people and serve them, because they think that they will lose something. They're afraid of paying out more than they get back, and being disempowered by the experience. It's almost as if there's only so much power to go around, and if they give some to someone else, there won't be as much left for them.

Nothing could be more untrue. Serving other people is one of the most empowering experiences in the world. We get infinitely more than we give, and the more we give, the more we get. Try it and see.

7. *Don't talk about the past.* Remember when you were younger and your grandparents used to say things like: "I remember when I was your age..." "Now, when *I* was young..." Did you find yourself rolling your eyes and starting to snore? Guess what. Younger people still do that.

When you start to talk about how things used to be in the good old days, it sounds is if: a) what's going on now isn't as valid, and b) you're finished and over the hill now, but back *then* you were important, and they'd better believe it. Would you want to be with a person like that?

Younger people turn off to talk like that. They fall asleep. It's boring to them. It's not inspiring or fun. Younger people aren't really the issue, however. The issue is that it keeps us stuck in the past, and that keeps us out of the here and now. We may have felt successful back then, and maybe we don't feel as successful now, but talking about nothing but how good it was in the good old days just perpetuates that situation.

I know a man who leads weekend seminars out in the country, and one of the ground rules is that no one can talk about anything that happened before they arrived Friday night. I'm not suggesting you do anything that extreme, but it's an interesting concept.

Words create realities. If you're always talking about the past, you'll stay stuck there. It's not that the past is bad, or that we shouldn't have rich memories. It's just that if that's all you think about, you miss some of the wonderful things that are happening here and now.

8. *Exercise.* Check with your doctor about what types and levels of exercise are best for you. Exercise, like standing up straight, moves your energy around and keeps it flowing, rather than static. Whenever something becomes static, it's in trouble.

Exercise is not only a way of feeling better, but a way of getting out and meeting people, of participating and expanding your circle of friends and activities.

Not only that, but we always look better when we exercises. It's wonderful not just for the shape of our bodies, but for our complexions and just about everything else. The best thing, though, is that it keeps us challenged and moving.

9. *Do things you've never done before.* You don't have to start a professional windsurfing career at the age of ninety-eight, but doing something new everyday is a tremendously invigorating experience.

It doesn't have to be a big thing. Buy a magazine you've never read. Take a walk you've never done. Eat a new food. Speak to someone you might not have spoken to before. Visit a new place.

It doesn't matter what you do, only that you do something new. It keeps life exciting, keeps you flexible and creative, and it's fun besides!

10. *Don't pretend you're younger than you are.* We've said a great deal about this in terms of physical things like tinting hair, but many people try to convey the impression when they talk that they're actually younger than they are. It's one thing for others simply to get the impression that we're younger, and quite another to try to convince them of it because we're ashamed of our age.

Age is nothing to be ashamed of. It's a badge of honor, especially if you've managed to avoid falling into the Polluted Pond. I think it's tremendously inspiring and invigorating to see someone who is eighty and still full of life and love. Those people are usually proud of their age, and actually find a way to let you know how old they are.

People always know what we're up to, whether or not they're conscious of knowing. If we're trying to hide something, they pick it up right away. They may not know exactly what it is, but they know that something is being hidden.

Trying to hide our age is a denial of who we are. I'm sixty, and I'm not about to try and convince people I'm younger. That would be exhausting! It's a losing battle anyway and besides, I have nothing to hide. I'm proud of the wisdom and experience I've accumulated over the years. I'd rather take a stand for being sixty and terrific than try to make people think I was forty.

11. *Live in the here and now.* Every moment is precious, a gift. What has gone before amounts to only memories. Memories are wonderful, but we can't live our lives around them. Living in the here and now keeps us vibrant, alive, interested and interesting. It's much more fun, and much more exciting.

Living in the here and now also helps overcome the "over there" syndrome, which suggests that things will be fine when...or...if...something happens that's not happening now. It's the old trap of wanting red hair when you have brown hair, brown hair when you have grey hair, so that you're never really quite satisfied with where you are. There's no end to it. It just goes on forever, so that you never get to be happy and satisfied.

Being in the here and now keeps us from thinking of ourselves as "former people" who used to be terrific but now are finished, just marking time. It lets us live fully, and that's what it's all about.

12. *Talk about your age...and tell the truth.* This business of women trying to keep their age a secret baffles me. Some women

go to great lengths to keep the secret, even trying to change their driver's licenses and birth records. Who do they think they're kidding? They are as attractive, or unattractive, as they are now no matter what numbers are after their name.

Even people who don't actively lie or go around forging public documents often try to avoid the subject. If confronted bluntly, they'll tell the truth, but they never bring up the subject themselves.

You don't have to buttonhole the first twenty people you see at a party and demand that they listen while you tell them your age, but there's no reason to avoid the subject. There's even some justification for bringing it up, especially if you talk about it in the context of being excited about "more life each year."

I find that, much as they hate to hear about "when I was your age," my young friends are actually fascinated by the idea of growing older without falling into the Polluted Pond. After all, some part of them must recognize that someday they will grow older, too. They think it's exciting that they don't have to do and be all the negative things they've been taught to associate with aging.

Talk about your age, and how excited you are to be enjoying it. They'll be green with envy.

13.  *Think positively*. With the Polluted Pond all around us, it's more important than ever to think positively. Don't accept negative ideas about growing older—or about anything—just because other people do. If you have a *lot* of friends who seem swamped with negativity, you might want to meet some new people.

Everyone can overcome negativity and false assumptions. Everyone can contribute to the world. Everyone can lead a fully exciting, meaningful life.

Age is wisdom, experience, richness...not retirement into oblivion and uselessness. You have a right to be in the world just exactly the way you are, and you can accomplish anything you set your mind to do.

Some people are lucky enough to be blessed with a naturally positive outlook. Others need to work at it a little. There are many ways to strengthen positive attitudes, and start to eliminate negative ones.

The first step is to identify both the positive and negative thoughts and attitudes that pop up most often. You might want to read over the positive list each day, just to remind yourself that you are basically an optimistic person and that these beliefs contribute to your positive reality. Then try to add to it. Each day, write down another positive thought or attitude that you adopt, or would like to adopt.

I wouldn't read over the negative list each day, because it may start to disappear on its own as you replace it with more and more positive thoughts and attitudes. It helps to be aware of what those negative thoughts are, though, so that you can watch out for them.

When things start going sour, when it seems as if everything is wrong and there's nothing you can do about it, look back and see which negative thoughts might be behind the situation. Don't beat yourself up. Just notice that you've been holding those negative thoughts, and then let go of them. If you can't be positive, at least put yourself into neutral. Then go back and read your positive list, and see if things don't start getting better.

14. *Stop competing.* It's bad enough when we're constantly comparing ourselves to our friends Betty or Sally, or to the people we see on the street. When we start comparing ourselves to the people in magazines or on TV, we're asking for trouble.

In the first place, a lot of us would look just that great if we'd had all the attention and artistry applied to us that's applied to those people.

In the second place, competing is a losing game. No one ever really wins. Each of us is unique. We all have our own special qualities, and they aren't meant to be sized up in relation to other people's special qualities. It's like trying to compare apples and oranges. They are two completely different things.

In the third place, it wouldn't hurt to give yourself a break. Life isn't a competition, a mine field waiting to explode in your face if you're not the most beautiful, the most talented, the most saintly. You are what you are. Relax and enjoy it.

15. *Remember to choose—minute to minute.* It's easy just to go along in life, waiting to see what happens to us. It's easy to take the point of view that things might be good, or they might be

bad. In any case, we have no control. We can only hope for the best. This is a road that leads directly to the Polluted Pond.

Life isn't always a bowl of cherries. There are difficult and uncomfortable times, but we always have a choice about how we're going to respond to them. We can knuckle under, give up and jump into the pond, or we can look at how we want things to be and take positive steps to turn them in that direction.

This road takes some courage. People tell us we can't do it, that we can't buck fate, that there's no way we can improve our situation. Often, these are the people who would rather just lie down on the railroad tracks themselves, and let life run over them. The last thing they want is to be accountable for their lives. They'd rather be miserable than allow for the possibility that they could do anything about it, because then they'd *have* to do something—or have no one to blame but themselves.

It's much easier to blame other people or circumstances for the things that go "wrong" in our lives, but in the end it's just not true. In the end, we are the choosers. We choose the people around us. We choose our approach to life and our response to individual situations. We choose our level of self-esteem.

It's a little more challenging than just rolling over and being victims, but it's also a lot more rewarding. It makes life fun and creative, rather than something to be endured.

16. *Choose carefully about tinting your hair or having plastic surgery.* These are serious matters. Coloring your hair may not be as potentially dangerous to your health as surgery, but its effects can be just as long-lasting. You may be letting yourself in for a lifetime of coloring, with all the time, expense and trouble that it entails—or at the very least, for a very unpleasant year of "growing out."

If you've seriously looked at the alternatives and are going to color your hair not because you're afraid of looking "old" or "mousey," then go ahead and have fun with it. Just be sure always to choose a color close to your own. There are wonderful preparations now and, if it's really what you want, you should be happy with it. I always like to make sure, however, that people are going *toward* something, and not *away* from it.

Many of these same principles apply to plastic surgery. I know women who think the thing you do the day after your fiftieth, or fortieth, birthday is to go out and have a face lift. They do it without even thinking, and that just doesn't make sense. Would you go in and have your hands or feet cut open without giving it some serious thought?

I've seen women get face lifts and actually look older, even though the surgery was successful and did just what they'd planned. It wasn't that their faces looked less smooth, but that they'd had the surgery done because they were terrified of growing older—and it showed. It showed through the smooth face, the tinted hair, and even through the beautiful clothes, because they hadn't done anything about their attitudes.

That's why doing surgery because of fear of looking older doesn't always produce the results people want. They get smoother faces and fewer wrinkles, but they still look scared and that makes them less attractive.

I've seen women who chose not to have surgery who look young, free and happy even though they have a lot of lines on their faces. They project a sense of themselves that's far more important than the number of wrinkles on their faces.

Remember, I'm not saying you should never have plastic surgery. It can do wonderful things. All I'm saying is to be sure and *choose*, and not have it done as a matter of course or because you're running away from something.

17. *Avoid getting into a rut.* It's easy, especially as we get older, to make do with what we have in terms of friends and activities. It seems like so much trouble to go out and meet new people, and sometimes it is! What we forget when we're sitting home by the fire is how exciting and rewarding it can be to bring new people into our lives. This is particularly true if our old friends aren't as supportive or stimulating as they used to be, or if for some reason they don't like it when we move and grow.

This doesn't mean we drop all our old friends. We can be just as close with them as ever—possibly more so, because we're able to bring more to the relationship. We'll always be there for them, but that doesn't mean we can't keep on growing. Our old friends and new friends might enjoy one another as well.

New activities can also be a source of joy and growth. I love learning new things, and doing things I've never done before, even if it's something as small as walking or driving to work a new way. It's fun, interesting, and gives me a sense of my own ability, my flexibility, and my confidence in handling new situations.

18. *Be yourself.* Start letting yourself do and say things you've always wanted to do and say. The freedom is exhilarating. Be more of yourself each day.

We're always afraid of what people will think of us, afraid they won't like us if we're just ourselves. In fact, just the opposite is often true. (If it's not, those might be friendships you want to examine more closely.) People are usually intrigued when we step out and do fun things. They want to be around us not only because it's exciting, but because then *they* can be more of themselves.

Trust your own instincts. They're your greatest strength. If we can't trust our instincts, we're just automatons.

19. *Don't use age as an excuse.* The quality of your life doesn't have to be determined by the number of years after your name. Just because you're a certain age doesn't mean you can't:
- exercise
- try new things
- wear certain colors
- act in certain ways
- be with certain people
- contribute to other people
- have as much fun and satisfaction in life as anyone else

Life is only over when we let it be.

20. *Create and express your own personal essence.* Whether it means having your colors done, seeing a someone who can advice you on line, texture, hair, makeup and clothing, or just sitting down with a piece of paper and looking at how you'd like your life to be, take some action that opens the door for you to express yourself more fully and creatively in the world.

Let it rip. Think about what you'd like your style to be, some new ways you'd like to express yourself, some new presence or part of yourself you'd like to show the world. Just thinking about it will start the ball rolling.

21. *Commit to more life each year.* All these ideas and suggestions are wonderful, but they don't do any good at all unless we do something with them. Some of them are challenging, even difficult. They stretch us. We aren't going to do some of them without a commitment.

Commitment to more life each year means that you, and you alone, are going to do whatever is necessary to feel more alive, beautiful and creative each year...each month...even each day. We all know that "no one can do it for us," and that's especially true in this case.

Living more fully each year isn't something you can accomplish by making a list of "to do's" and faithfully running down it and checking them off. It's a way of looking at life and at yourself. It's a way of letting yourself experience the goodness that already exists around you, of giving up negativity from both internal and external sources, and of taking the reins of your life into your own hands.

It's not always easy to remember that we have a choice. Sometimes it takes simply adopting the point of view that we do, even when we're not entirely convinced of it, and then operating in life from that premise—over and over again.

When people do that, it isn't long before it becomes very real to them. They realize that there is no situation in which they don't have a choice—at least about their response—and the result is almost always a tremendous surge of personal power and of compassion for others.

It's one of the most amazing things I've ever seen. People who had been powerless, even helpless, suddenly come into a quiet sense that they are the masters of their own destiny. They start doing things they didn't think they could do, and having all sorts of new experiences. People want to be with them. They have become bigger than they were, and have even more love.

These are only a few of the things you can do to avoid the Polluted Pond and live more life each year. You can probably think of many more, and the ones you come up with will probably be the most valuable for you.

Some may seem too silly or uncomfortable at first, but once you start, it will be hard to stop. Once you take that first step, and make a commitment to more life each year, they will get easier and easier, more and more fun. Soon, the things on this list will seem like child's play and you'll have to come up with more.

Be creative with this list. Add your own ideas. Then start doing them!

## 10.
## "MORE LIFE" EXERCISE

In the course of this book, we have suggested several exercises to help you stay clear of the Polluted Pond, live more life each year, and feel beautiful in the process.

In this chapter, we have gathered them all together so that you can dip into them anytime you feel tempted to take a stroll along the edges of the pond and think you might just fall in, or anytime you simply feel like doing something positive. You can dip into this reservoir and choose whichever exercises you like.

One reason we haven't made a big deal of them in the individual chapters is that I hate feeling that I can't go on to the next chapter, or that I can't get full benefit out of the next chapter unless I've done the exercise. It becomes like homework—something I *have* to do, something that is probably boring, distasteful and awful.

I don't want you to approach these exercises that way. If you never do any of them, fine. You'll still get the full value from this book. They're just here if you feel like doing them and if they appeal to you. Those are probably the only circumstances under which they'll be of real value to you anyway.

There's no particular order in which you should do these exercises. The best way is to see which one looks like most fun, or which one resonates with you. That's the one that will be most valuable.

There's also no particular *way* to do these exercises. When people tell me I have to do a certain drill or exercise five minutes everyday or forget it, I usually forget it. If these exercises ever become an ordeal for you, I suggest you stop doing them. Life is not about being miserable, and neither is this book. Do them as much as you feel like, but don't *not* do them because you think you're not doing them right, or think you're not doing them often enough. There's no right way, and no right amount of time.

Do them when you can. Realize that the more you do them,

the more benefits you'll get, but don't beat yourself up for not making them a full-time job. If you want to spend five seconds on one of these exercises three days a week, that's a lot better than not doing it at all, and probably better than doing it for a long period of time if you resent having to put in the time. Create your own pace.

Please feel free to modify the exercises. If you like one, but want to change it a little, go ahead. They're for you, to do with whatever you want. Do whatever is going to work for you. We're going for results here, not an investment of time. You can even do some of them while you're driving in the car.

Here they are. Take your pick.

#1.   YOUR IDEAL SELF. Imagine what you would be like if you were exactly the way you wanted to be—not necessarily physically (although this is a powerful exercise, too), but mentally, spiritually, emotionally. How would you relate to yourself and to other people? Your mate? Your children? Your work? Your friends? Your physical environment? What kinds of things would you do? Say? Think? Be? What presence or inner essence would you project into the world? What kinds of clothing would you wear?

My reaction when I first did this exercise was, "I could never reach that, ever!" I was amazed to find that the more I did this exercise, the more quickly that ideal person actually became a part of me, and I a part of her. I found myself doing things that she would do, thinking the way she would think, and actually becoming the "me" I've always wanted to be.

In a couple of years, I was actually that person. Then I could start all over and extend a little further. I think the magic of this exercise comes from the fact that the ideal person is already inside us. She has to be, or else we couldn't imagine her. Anything we can imagine, we can become.

This is one of the most powerful exercises I've found, and is just as valuable at eighty as it is at fifteen.

#2.   MIRROR. Look at yourself in the mirror, but not the way you've ever looked before. Start at the top of your head and work down from your hair to your forehead, eyebrows, eyes, nose, checks, mouth, chin, neck, shoulders, etc.

Notice some of the negative decisions that come up. Don't believe them, but just notice that they are there. See what decisions you've made about each part of yourself, then check to see if that decision still has any validity. More often than not, it's something you decided when you were quite young and has nothing to do with you now.

Then go back and see yourself through new eyes, as if you'd never made that decision. You may even want to make an affirmation that's different from the decision, and change the pattern of your thinking. You might want to affirm, for instance, "It is now time for my body to be thin (healthy, energetic, etc.)!"

If you thought your eyes were too close together, you might want to say aloud or to yourself, "My eyes are perfectly placed. They're my way of experiencing the world and serve me well. They let my inner beauty shine through to the world."

Do this with your whole body, but particularly with the parts of yourself that haven't been your friends in the past. As you affirm positive thoughts about yourself and your appearance, you can almost see the change in the physical reality.

It doesn't have to take a long time. You can do it while you're drying your hair. Many women have told me they dry their hair with no clothes on so they can do this exercise at the same time.

Here are the steps again:
1. Look in the mirror.
2. Notice what you don't like.
3. See what decision you make about that part.
4. Check to see if it's still valid. (The chances are it's not.)
5. Change your thought pattern with a positive affirmation or imagery.

#3. PARK BENCH. Close your eyes and imagine that you are sitting on a park bench. You look over and see a person sitting on the opposite bench, and it's YOU. See what that person looks like. Be objective. Do this exercise as if you weren't talking about yourself, but about a stranger.

What would you say about that person? Tell yourself about her. What does she represent to you? What presence does she project?

When you're finished, let go of all your thoughts and images.

The purpose of this exercise is not to see yourself as particularly positive or negative, but simply to see how you DO see yourself, so that you can go on from there and create a new reality if you wish…or simply appreciate the old one more.

#4. PARTY. You're at a party where you don't know anyone. Suddenly you see two people you know, and they are talking to one another. You move toward them, but as you come close you hear your name and realize that they are talking about you.

What are they saying? What do they think of you?

#5. THE FIRST DECISION. Choose a quiet time when you won't be disturbed and try to recall the first negative decision you made about yourself. It probably happened when you were quite young, so you may have to go back in time. If you feel comfortable doing so, close your eyes and see what decision comes up. Then try to find an earlier one. When did you make it? When did you start buying that you weren't perfect? What was the incident? What was the year?

When you've found the earliest negative decision you can, check to see if it is still true. The chances are it's not, and if you can let go of that first negative decision, you may crumble a whole stack of them.

I've seen people find it, and have many, many other negative decision simply fall away. This is rare, and you shouldn't expect it to happen overnight, but it's an enormous help to find that first decision.

#6. FIVE-SECOND MEDITATION. Sometime during the day, take just five seconds to close your eyes and flash on how your body and face would look if they were just the way you wanted them to be.

Create an image in your mind. Experience all the wonderful feelings you feel as you exist in that body and face. Then let go and return to whatever you were doing. This exercise is one of the most powerful you can do.

#7. THE BALLS OF YOUR FEET. Someone said, if you can feel the balls of your feet, you are conscious of living in a body. That may sound silly at first, but it's amazing how many people walk around not really aware that they are living in bodies. They know they're not ghosts, of course, but they're not really aware of how their body feels, what signals it's giving them, the pleasure it allows them, or the fact that it needs some attention.

Remember the balls of your feet, remember that you have the gift of a body, and remember that it's the place you live!

#8. DRIVING. I can get sloppy about my posture when I drive, so I've started being very conscious of sitting up straight behind the wheel. You can think up a lot of tricks to make yourself more aware of your posture. Everytime you look at the gas gauge, or the speedometer, look at how you are sitting as well. Then line up your head, neck, shoulders, trunk and stomach. It will carry over to your standing posture.

#9. RUBBER BAND. If there's anything you want to change about yourself, or anything you want to remember to be conscious of, put a rubber band around your wrist and snap it gently from time to time.

Most things we want to change are just habits, whether they're physical habits like smoking or negative thought patterns. You might have the habit, for instance, of thinking your thighs are too big. Each time you catch yourself thinking that, snap the rubber band gently and reprogram. And each time you become aware of the rubber band, think to yourself, "My thighs aren't really so big."

Use this technique however it works best for you, but take advantage of the physical reminder, and the gentle snapping that actually sends messages to your brain so you can reprogram your thoughts. You can do this with anything you want to rechoose about or rethink.

These are only a few of the many exercise you can use to become more beautiful, healthier, and more alive. Others will occur to you as you start doing these, and the ones that occur to you will probably be the most valuable.

Make these exercises your own by modifying them in any way that works for you, and be on the lookout for more.

Most important of all, delight in each minute that you spend doing them. They are for you, a way of nurturing yourself, having fun, and becoming more of who you are. Enjoy!

## 11.
## WRAPPING IT UP

*Form and Substance*

We've talked about many things in this book. Some of them have to do with physical realities, and those I like to call "form." Others have to do with attitudes and ways of being, and those I like to call "substance." The two work together. It's very difficult to have one without the other.

Beautiful substance leads to beautiful form, and beautiful form reflects beautiful substance. Together, they lead to more life each year, more joy in living, and more creative expression of your own unique essence. *Looking great is a vital part of who you are.*

Deepening and appreciating our substance is tremendously important no matter what our age. It is the basis of our beauty. It's made of things like our experience of living, our love of life, our deepening wisdom. The more adept we become at letting our substance shine through, the more beauty we create around us to enjoy and share with others—our families, coworkers and friends.

Sometimes we ourselves are the last to see and appreciate that special beauty that grows within us each year we are on earth. I hope that this book has opened some doors to that appreciation. There are many things we can do to enjoy more life each year, but the foundation on which they all rest is our own self-esteem, our sense of ourselves as valuable, beautiful, expressive people who have a right to be all that we can be.

For me, it all comes down to the Seven Secrets of Aging Beautifully. Remembering them, perhaps even reading them over each day, makes everything else fall into place. Here's a quick review.

### THE SEVEN SECRETS TO AGING BEAUTIFULLY

1. *Accept and love yourself.* Let go of diminising thoughts and opinions about yourself, self-criticism and feelings that you aren't all right just the way you are. Without self-love and self-acceptance, it's difficult to do anything else. This is the cornerstone of your relationship with yourself and with everyone else.

2. *Don't buy into the Polluted Pond.* Examine each issue of "aging" separately, and don't buy the whole pond if it isn't true

for you. You have a choice about whether or not to buy in. Check out any payoffs you may be getting and, if they're not worth it, make a commitment to stay away from the pond.

3.  *Concentrate on your natural perfection, resonance and harmony, rather than on faults or imperfections.* Look at yourself with a new focus. Each of us is a part of nature, as uniquely beautiful as a sunset or flower. When we look to that, rather than picking ourselves apart, then our individual beauty comes to the surface and becomes what we and others see.

4.  *Remember that you're in charge.* Your attitudes shape your age, your level of aliveness, and the amount of joy and grace you find in living. You are holding the reins, and can go in any direction you choose. It's your life, and you choose to be any way you want.

5.  *Be open to a variety of styles and ideas, and be willing to stay current.* Have fun trying new things. Don't get stuck in the past, whether it's some particular time in your life or just old ideas. Being flexible gives you confidence to meet new challenges, and the assurance that you'll always keep growing.

6.  *Take a stand for yourself.* Trust yourself and your instincts. Tell the truth about yourself, be true to yourself, and let the chips fall where they may. If people don't like what you're doing, it's their problem. Don't waste your life by not being all of who you are.

7.  *Create your possibilities; don't limit them.* You can do either. It's all in your hands. Creating possibilities, opportunities and new expressions of yourself leads to more life, more expansion, more happiness. Limiting possibilities leads to stagnation.

You probably know some secrets yourself. This is only a beginning. Living by these principles can be a first step to opening up possibilities you've never dreamed of, finding parts of yourself you thought you lost long ago or that you never knew you had, expressing a depth of yourself that brings tremendous joy to you and those close to you.

I invite you to share in all that, to go beyond where you have been, to start exploring and expressing yourself in new ways, and to enjoy what being on earth is all about—more life each year.